"The fight against racism  ceptions and assumptior... *Man's Journey to Desegre... ... vividly depicts the cultural, ethnic, and racial make-up of a biracial man's life. Devin Hughes tells his story with passion and fierce humanity."

KATHIA FLEMENS, PhD
GEORGE WASHINGTON UNIVERSITY

"Somehow I know myself a little better for reading the memoirs of another man. Devin's story is moving, inspirational, and flat-out real. Knowing what it means to be black, white, or any other ethnicity is more confusing than it's been at any time in America's history. Through the lens of Devin's life, we can all take steps toward harmony with ourselves and our neighbors."

DONNIE BRYANT
AUTHOR AND COPYWRITER

"Devin takes the reader on a revealing life journey, which confirms the age-old adage to 'never judge a book by its cover.' His story is funny, sad, motivating, and thought provoking. It will cause you to pause and reflect on your life and your perceptions of others; you just never know what may be going on behind the scenes of other people's lives."

ERIK C. HARRIS
VICE PRESIDENT OF MARKETING, CRESCENDO BIOSCIENCE

"Devin Hughes has developed an inspiring and thought provoking autobiography that reminds us of the fragility of the human spirit, but also reinforces the importance of being comfortable in one's own skin while navigating the uncertain waters of today's globalized and highly competitive society. Hughes' story reminds us that no matter where we come from or what adversity we have faced, we can be successful and make a difference in the world."

CHRISTIAN TEETER, Ed.D
SECRETARY OF THE BOARD OF TRUSTEES, COAST COMMUNITY COLLEGE DISTRICT

DEVIN C. HUGHES
CONTRAST
A BIRACIAL MAN'S JOURNEY TO DESEGREGATE HIS PAST

CONTRAST: A BIRACIAL MAN'S JOURNEY TO DESEGREGATE HIS PAST

Writers of the Round Table Press
PO Box 511
Highland Park, IL 60035

Writers of the Round Table Press and logo are trademarks of Round Table Companies and Writers of the Round Table Inc.

Front cover design by Analee Paz
Interior design/layout and back cover by Sunny DiMartino

Printed in the United States of America

First Edition: June 2012
10 9 8 7 6 5 4 3 2 1

Library of Congress Cataloging-in-Publication Data

Hughes, Devin C.
Contrast: A Biracial Man's Journey to Desegregate His Past / Devin C. Hughes.—1st ed. p. cm.
ISBN 978-1-61066-054-9
Library of Congress Control Number 2012941334

CONTENTS

For my family and friends,
who see me just as Devin.

ACKNOWLEDGMENTS

I would like to thank Suzanne, my wife and best friend, for the patience she showed during endless conversations about this project. She watched me pace around the house and listened as I recounted my childhood to her, our four kids (Bailey, Skylar, Harper, and Finlay), and anyone else who offered an ear. This book would not have been possible without her support and encouragement. I am not sure I would be at this point in my life without her by my side.

Words cannot express my gratitude to my good friends at Round Table Companies, who did not just help me write a manuscript but embraced going on this journey with me. I thank Corey Michael Blake for his creativity and unbridled wit, coupled with his belief in my story as a catalyst to improve the planet; Erin Cohen for her support, humor, and faith in me; Kristin Westberg for being there in a pinch when I came calling with last-minute requests; and Nadja Baer, my staff editor, who was absolutely instrumental in bringing this book to life. An extra "shout out" to my executive editor, Katie Gutierrez, for her patience in dealing with my quirks and eclectic personality and for always being there to pick me up when I fell down. You're awesome, Katie! Finally, special thanks to my father, who helped shaped my story, my words, and my life.

GOVERNMENT OF THE DISTRICT OF COLUMBIA
DEPARTMENT OF HEALTH
CERTIFICATE OF LIVE BIRTH

DISTRICT OF COLUMBIA DEPARTMENT OF PUBLIC HEALTH
CERTIFICATE OF LIVE BIRTH

1969 JUN 24

BIRTH NO. 108—

69 12080

1. PLACE OF BIRTH

Washington, D. C.

Name of Hospital or Institution (If not in Hospital, give street address)
Sibley Memorial Hospital

2. USUAL RESIDENCE OF MOTHER (Where does mother live?)

State	County	City, Town, or Location
District of Col.	District of Columbia	Washington

Street Address: 2209 Randolph Street N.E.

Is Residence Inside City Limits? Yes ☒ No ☐
Is Residence on a Farm? Yes ☐ No ☒

CHILD

3. CHILD'S NAME (Type or Print)
(First) Devin (Middle) Chaise (Last) Hughes

4. SEX: Male ☒ Female ☐
5a. THIS BIRTH: Single ☒ Twin ☐ Triplet ☐
5b. IF TWIN OR TRIPLET (This child born) 1st ☐ 2nd ☐ 3rd ☐
6. DATE OF BIRTH (Month) June (Day) 6 (Year) 1969

FATHER OF CHILD

7. NAME (First) Clarkie (Middle) Reed (Last) Hughes
8. COLOR OR RACE Negro
9. AGE (At time of this birth) 34 YEARS
10. BIRTHPLACE (State or foreign country) S.C.
11a. USUAL OCCUPATION Produce Manager
11b. KIND OF BUSINESS OR INDUSTRY A&P Tea Company

MOTHER OF CHILD

12. MAIDEN NAME (First) Gloria (Middle) Charlotte (Last) French
13. COLOR OR RACE White
14. AGE (At time of this birth) 18 YEARS
15. BIRTHPLACE (State or foreign country) Tenn.
16. CHILDREN PREVIOUSLY BORN TO THIS MOTHER (Do NOT include this child)
a. How many OTHER children are now living? 0
b. How many OTHER children were born alive but are now dead? 0
c. How many children were still born (born dead after 20 weeks pregnancy)? 0

17. INFORMANT (Mother) Mrs. Gloria Hughes

I hereby certify that this child was born alive on the date stated above at the hour of 7:23 A.M.

18. SIGNATURE _____ M.D.
ADDRESS 755 ____
19. DATE SIGNED ____ 40/69

NAME Mrs. Clarkie Hughes
ADDRESS 2209 Randolph Street N.E.
CITY Washington STATE D.C.

Full name of child should read: Devin Chaise Hughes.
Added from sup. 8-4-69

DC246597

DATE ISSUED
February 22, 2001

Earl W. Wilson
Carl W. Wilson, Registrar

Devin's birth certificate

Devin's parents

Devin and his father

Devin and his parents

INTRODUCTION
LEAVING THE RACIAL WITNESS PROTECTION PROGRAM

Throughout my life, relationships have been transient.
My parents fled the dangerous bigotry of the South in
1960s, leaving their families behind for good; as a result,
I had little to no connection with my extended family.
The friends I made in elementary school were forgotten
by the time I started middle school. I had close friends
in high school whom I never spoke to again after graduation. I conditioned myself to enjoy relationships when I
had them, and if they went, they went. It was like reading a book and burning each chapter as I completed it,
remembering but not integrating it with the chapter
to come.

The inability to connect to people around me
stemmed, in large part, from my inability to connect to
my own identity. You can't be present in the moment
with others if you are not comfortable with who you are
as a person. As a biracial child, I tried for years to de-
fine myself via race, but I didn't know which one I was.
From childhood through college, I viewed the world
from lower-middle class, black eyes—the eyes of my
father. I used black vernacular, and I didn't trust white
people. After I graduated college in May of 1991, I went
into the witness protection program, so to speak, about
my racial makeup. I have been there until now.

In some ways, maintaining secrecy about my background has been like spying. With the light skin, "good"

hair, and green eyes of my mother, I've felt like a CIA agent in hostile territory, cooperating, collaborating, and cohabitating with folks who don't know my background. One reason I've kept quiet is silent protest: why should I have to tell people I was mixed? Why did race have to enter the equation at all? Was I supposed to carry around an index card with my DNA on it and share it with everyone I met? At this point in my life, I'm tired of the secrecy, tired of pretending, tired of playing the social chameleon. If people don't know who you are, you can't let your guard down and establish an authentic connection.

It's a new thing for me, opening up to people around me and reaching out to those who drifted from my life years ago. I reconnected with folks from high school in DC, with whom I played basketball and who are predominantly black. It felt good to reestablish those bonds, both with the people and that part of my heritage, so I started an alumni association for my high school basketball program. I have also organized an annual reunion event. It's a catalyst to get people back together, but for me it plays a much bigger role: it's a step toward integrating past and present, black and white.

If the racial divide I've struggled to overcome in myself echoes the larger conversation of race in this country, it is an impediment to moving forward. As a society, we have become so PC that most people are afraid to broach the race topic, even when the intent may be a better mutual understanding. Someone has to make the first move, let down the guard, open up. I'm finally willing to do that.

As a happily married father of four, and an entrepreneur, I'm looking for meaning, not money. I want my legacy to be an impetus for change. My hope is that this isn't the kind of book you read once and put away. I hope you reach for it when you need motivation to connect with your identity or reason to ignite a conversation with others in your life who feel unsure, ambiguous, or disconnected. I hope my story encourages you to move forward … while never completely discarding what you leave behind.

CHAPTER 1

LOVE, SUPPLANTED

"LITTLE RED NIGGER," MY FATHER'S FAMILY SNEERED.

Dad was born in Mullins, South Carolina, in 1935 to an absentee father and an alcoholic mother. With a lack of real parental figures, he spent much of his childhood with his uncle, aunt, and cousins; life wasn't much better there. He wasn't referred to by name but rather the lighter color of his skin next to theirs. They made his color something to be ashamed of, though my father secretly felt they were envious. Even as a child, he recognized that skin was not just skin.

By the age of nine, Dad was essentially on his own. Segregation was a part of his daily life. He used separate bathrooms and school water fountains from whites, and he needed to be off the streets before the seven o'clock curfew. One of his aunts did the laundry for the Ku Klux Klan—shocking to me, the idea of washing those white hoods for the very people who would lynch folks like her, but my dad said that was life; you just made do. When he was ten, he was molested by one of his older cousins. Under the same philosophy, he kept it to himself.

Growing up, there were many things I didn't know about my father. For example, I never knew the story of how he met my mother.

At sixteen, Dad joined the U.S. Air Force. He went through basic training, and nine months passed before anyone discovered he was underage. At that point, he was kicked out. A year later, this time with parental consent, Dad re-enlisted and fought in the Korean War. After too much drinking one night, he thought his best friend was trying to put the moves on his girlfriend, and he shot the guy in the leg. His friend was fine, but my father spent two years in the brig.

As a kid, I was intrigued by the image of my father in lockdown. I envisioned a bunch of tough guys all out for themselves, trading, hustling, stealing, lying, testing one another for weaknesses like a pack of wolves waiting to devour the weakest link. I couldn't imagine how my dad survived in any kind of prison, let alone military prison, but his strategy was to act like a lunatic so no one would mess with him. His first crazy act was to find one of the biggest, toughest guys in the place and punch him in the mouth. That wild, "do anything" reputation was necessary for his survival; at five-eleven and one hundred and sixty pounds, my dad didn't know of any other way to ensure his safety. He built up a network of other inmates and emerged as a leader; even in prison, people needed someone to call the shots.

While in prison, he befriended the son of George Roby Dempster, former mayor of Knoxville and the inventor of the Dempster-Dumpster. Dempster's son was timid and allegedly homosexual. My father was empathetic to anyone who couldn't defend himself, especially those who were victimized for identities they couldn't change. He became a surrogate brother to this rich, entitled white kid, protecting him from those who would take advantage of him. That friendship led to my father moving to Knoxville after prison; his new friend had gotten him a job with Dempster Construction Company, his father's business, giving my dad an opportunity to start over after his bad conduct discharge.

My father hated his job at Dempster. The segregation

of his youth continued at the job site. White workers operated heavy machinery, while black workers had to shovel or do other hard manual labor. Due to his relationship with the owner's son, my father was allowed to work with some of the heavy equipment. The favoritism others thought he received branded him as an "uppity nigger."

While working at Dempster Construction Company, my father met a woman named Ella. They dated briefly, and Ella became pregnant. He wasn't in love with her, but they got married because he felt it was the right thing to do. He hadn't had much of a home life as a child, and he didn't want to create more dysfunction. They named their son Marty and, five years later, had a daughter they called Tracy.

My father worked at Dempster for five years before finding a new job with the local A&P grocery store. He worked there for three years before meeting a part-time employee named Gloria … my mother.

He was thirty-three and married with two kids under the age of ten. She was a seventeen-year-old white girl, a homecoming queen who had been accepted to the University of Tennessee. With red hair and green eyes, she was attractive and popular, but she rebelled against her controlling parents. She routinely flirted with my father, and her smile and her magnetic personality piqued his interest. Her boundless energy and outgoing personality made him feel young. They began sneaking out to be together, and they fell in love. When her parents discovered she was running around with a black man sixteen years her senior, all hell broke loose.

Her father started to follow them around, carrying a gun. He stopped by the bars my father frequented, looking for him. My parents were both scared; an interracial affair wasn't just illicit but dangerous during those days. At a bar one night, her father bragged to his buddies that if my father didn't disappear, he would *make* him disappear. At that point, my parents decided to escape to Washington, DC.

My mother moved first. Even though she was white, I imagine her as a slave in the Civil War era, fleeing from the Deep South to the liberated north, where she could live without fear. She would be moving in with my dad's Aunt Fanny, whom I imagined as one of the members of the Underground Railroad, furtively helping to shuttle persecuted slaves northward.

After she left, Mom called her mother and let her know she was no longer in Tennessee; she didn't feel safe there, she said. Her parents tried convincing her to come home, and when she refused, they said, "That's it. You're done." They cut her from their lives, and I'm not sure she ever stopped feeling abandoned.

Aunt Fanny's house provided a place of respite where my mother could recalibrate. The house was far different from the Tennessee farm where she'd grown up. Except for my dad, she'd rarely spent time with black people; now she was living with them in a tight house filled with kids. She was also transitioning from living at home, as a child being taken care of by parents, to being an adult.

While my mom waited for my dad, she did a lot of soul searching. She was eighteen or nineteen; what did she want from this new future she'd jumped into? She was obviously not enrolling in the University of Tennessee, so what would she do for work? She took some odd jobs while searching for a place to live, but most of her effort was spent getting her bearings. There was a lot of uncertainty, and the realities were harsh, especially with not having my father—the catalyst in all this—by her side. He said he would join her, but would he really? She felt alone on an island.

In Tennessee, my father kept working as he tried to figure out his next steps. He communicated regularly with my mother and Aunt Fanny, but there was a lot of chaos during that time. It was a year before he left his kids and wife, who later moved to San Diego to be closer to Ella's sister. Initially, he had wanted to move the whole family out of Tennessee, so that he could be with my mother and still be a father to his first two children, but his wife refused. Dad essentially missed his other kids' whole lives, but he never owns any of that. He says Ella wouldn't let him be a part of their lives, though he faithfully paid child support all those years. His temper is quick when the subject is raised, and I'm sure it's not based purely on anger; guilt and remorse play a role as well.

When my parents were finally together in DC, their lives remained uncertain. They were in an unfamiliar place, trying to get their roots to take hold under them. At first, they were happy. They had gotten away from all the negativity in the south and were starting over. My father was able to transfer to a new job with A&P, and my mother was trying to figure out what she wanted to do. Within a year, a justice of the peace married them in a simple ceremony, and they began the transition from secretly dating to living together as husband and wife. They were naïve; their romanticized notion of "the North" didn't exist. They weren't prepared for the hard stares of strangers.

In Dad's first week at the new A&P, my mom went to visit him at the store. He gave her a hug, and she smiled as she left his side to wander into the aisles. One hand rested on her obviously pregnant stomach as she walked away. Before she returned, one of the managers approached my father.

"Who's that white girl you're with?" he asked.

"That's my wife," Dad said, smiling but instinctively defensive.

The only response he received was an appalled, shocked look.

Within a few weeks, my father was talking to the store leadership about wanting to move up; he was excited to be in the DC area, and he wanted to be a manager someday. The answer that came back was, "You're never going to be a manager here married to some white woman." The news dealt a knockout emotional blow to my father. He worked for A&P for thirty-nine years, the majority of which he spent in the produce section of that store in DC. Toward the end of his career, he began working the checkout lanes, but he never did make manager.

After I was born, life continued to be a struggle for my parents. Mom found work as a receptionist and file clerk at a physician's office during the day. They had to work a lot of hours to support the three of us. Aunt Fanny was not an option for a babysitter; Dad didn't think it was a suitable environment for an infant, with all the late-night traffic Fanny's sons brought through the house.

"People don't want to help a couple like us," Dad said to one of his coworkers as they stacked a display of cauliflower. "But what are we supposed to do with a kid when we both have to work to support us?"

"Well, what about your families?"

"What families?" Dad said bluntly.

"Excuse me," a large black woman broke into their conversation.

"Can I help you?" Dad asked.

She held out her hand. "My name is Lela. I overheard you say you're looking for a babysitter."

CHAPTER 2

EARLY INCONGRUENCE

DAD DROVE ME TO LELA'S FOR MY FIRST BABYSITTING EXPERIENCE. Mom hadn't gotten home from the night shift yet, and he had to be at the grocery store before seven a.m. to unload the morning delivery. It was still dark out, but the sky had started to lighten at its edges. Streetlamps flickered outside my window. I sat in the back seat without a seatbelt. My legs stuck straight out in front of me and my feet bounced at every bump in the road. I held on to the armrest in the door to keep from sliding on the turns. A few minutes into the drive, I was bored. I hauled myself over the top of the seat in front of me and slid sideways into the front.

"What do you think you're doing?" Dad asked, a big smile on his face.

I pushed some of the buttons on the dash. "Where are we going?"

"Nowhere. We're not going anywhere until you get in the back seat."

I pulled myself up, using the headrest as a handhold. The car went over a bump and I lost my grip. I tumbled onto the floor behind Dad. The carpet felt gritty. I clambered back up onto the seat.

"Where are we going?" I asked again.

"Lela's house. She's going to watch you while we're at work," Dad said. He looked at me in the rearview mirror. "She's nice. You can watch TV or play."

I yawned. I was nervous about being left at a stranger's house, but I was tired. I dozed off on the way there. The next thing I knew, the car door was open and Dad shook me awake.

"We're here, Devin."

I slowly climbed down out of the seat and followed close behind Dad. His Buick sat parked behind a clean, shiny Cadillac. Lela's neighborhood didn't look like ours. Rows of one- and two-story brick houses sat behind sidewalks and neatly manicured lawns. Here, the tree-lined streets were quiet. Everything looked neat and clean; there was no garbage spilling out of dumpsters or floating through the gutters. The only cars I saw were parked in short driveways instead of on the streets. There were no parking lots. Before now, I hadn't ever met black people who owned their own houses. The morning air felt crisp and cool.

"You're going to love it," Dad tried to convince me. He rang the doorbell. "She's been a nanny before, so she has a lot of toys for you to play with."

I hid behind Dad when the door swung open a few moments later. A mid-fifties, heavyset black woman peered out at us behind huge glasses; at first glance, she reminded me of Aunt Fanny. As soon as I saw her looking at me, I grabbed Dad's pant leg as tight as I could and buried my face in it. I waited for the snappy barrage of questions that Aunt Fanny fired at me every time she saw me: "Are you happy, boy? Why don't you smile? Are you being a good boy?"

"He'll be all right," I heard the woman reassure Dad as he tried to peel my arms apart. "It's natural for him to be afraid."

Despite my best efforts to dig my fingernails into his leg, Dad disentangled himself from my grip. "Have fun. I'll pick you up when I get off work later." With that, I was left in the entryway of this woman's house as her front door closed behind Dad.

For a moment, we stood there quietly. All the furniture beyond her looked worn but in good condition. The floors were clean. The house had a good feeling to it, as if people laughed here. I had to lean my head back to look up at Lela. She wore a long, flower-print skirt and a grandmotherly sweater buttoned over her shoulders, the sleeves hanging down the sides of her arms.

"Have you had breakfast yet?" she asked me.

I shook my head.

"That's something we'll have to fix, then, isn't it?" She reached out her hand. I took it and followed her to the kitchen.

Lela was so heavy that she couldn't move gracefully. She lumbered, leaning from side to side and bumping into me every few steps. Once I was settled in a chair, she opened a cupboard and took out a box of Cream of Wheat. She ran water into a pot in the sink, busying herself making me a hot breakfast. I sat and watched in awe: someone was cooking for me. Just for me. Minutes later, I had a bowl of steaming hot cereal with a bit of sugar sitting in front of me.

I stirred the strange concoction with my spoon. A hearty, comforting smell rose from the bowl. Maybe this wouldn't be so bad, I thought, leaning into the steam. After all, no one ever made me a hot breakfast at home. At most, Mom plopped down a bowl of cold cereal before grabbing her own meal and disappearing into her bedroom. I chanced a smile at Lela.

After I ate, I explored the house a little. I had never been in a house with stairs. *This must be what it's like to have a real home,* I thought as I looked up toward the second floor. The steps were too steep for my short legs, so I crawled up as best I could, using my arms to stabilize and pull myself onto the next one. Lela watched over me but didn't interrupt. At the top, I turned around and made my way back down the same way, leaning on my arms while my legs searched for a foothold below. I spent an hour going up and down with no purpose except to experience the feeling of being in a house.

I fell in love with Lela quickly. Unlike my mom, who spent her days either working or sleeping, Lela actively looked for ways to engage with me. She taught me how to play jacks, kept a close eye on me when I played by myself, and involved me in conversation even when we watched TV. Three times a day, I sat at her kitchen table and watched her cook me meals. I wondered if she thought in advance about what she was going to make me, if she made lists and took them to the grocery store. I couldn't imagine someone putting in that much effort for me, and doing so with a smile. I gravitated toward Lela's attention, but at four years old, I didn't know which was normal: her way of caring for me or my mother's more distanced affection.

Lela was also a gifted storyteller. It became a ritual for her to sit in a recliner while I lay back on the stairs I loved so much. Her chair was turned sideways, so she didn't look at me directly, but that didn't matter. Her voice had a soothing quality, low and reverberating. Sometimes she read out loud from books—classic stories like *Jack and the Beanstalk* that I had never heard of—and sometimes she made up her own while she knitted. I propped my head up on my arm, entranced by the way her hands and words weaved complicated patterns.

This ritual felt like a natural part of the day. She never walked in and said, "It's story time," before beginning. It was more like she was in the driver's seat and I had stowed away in the back for a fantastical road trip to unknown destinations. I never interrupted her; that would be like calling attention to myself in the backseat and risking turning around and going home. I didn't want to go home.

Some of Lela's stories centered on a young man who had to overcome extraordinary circumstances but eventually triumphed by graduating college and becoming successful. Others were about families having to work together to overcome the father losing his job, or about kids who made a lot of friends because they were nice, well mannered, and treated all people fairly. I didn't realize it, but she must have been trying to build a connection between her characters and me.

"You see, Devin," she often said at the end of each narrative, "when you fall down, you have to get right back up and try again. No excuses."

I nodded solemnly.

Lela and her husband had a couple of children of their own, but they were grown and out of the house. Her husband worked during the day, so I didn't see him often. He wore suits and carried a briefcase. I didn't know what his job was, but it was enough to afford a house and a Cadillac, so they must have done something right. The *what if's* floated through my head. What if my dad wore a suit? What if Mom read me stories? What if we lived in a house like this? Could we have this same, peaceful life?

I knew my parents loved me, but they had other things going on in their lives—work that made their voices tense, friends who sometimes filled the house on weekends. At Lela's, I was the most important thing; she was one hundred percent focused on me. Every time I left, I couldn't wait to go back.

Lela taught me skills that my parents didn't have time to teach me. Dad didn't try to teach me manners; Mom tried sometimes, but between working two jobs and sleeping, she didn't have much energy. Simple things, like turning off the lights and closing a door when I left a room, washing my hands after using the restroom and saying please and thank-you, were all things I learned from Lela.

One day at lunch, she decided I was ready to learn how to use silverware properly. My chair was scooted so close to the kitchen table that my chest pressed into the edge. I had the end of my fork clenched in my fist and was trying to navigate the tines to my mouth. By this time, I had strewn macaroni and cheese all over the table around my plate. Lela grabbed a damp rag from the sink and ambled over to my chair. After wiping up my mess, she pulled the fork out of my hand.

"Here," she said. "Like this." I felt her reassuring presence above me as she leaned over and put her arms around mine. She demonstrated where I should put my fingers, and then put her hand over mine to show me. "See?"

"Yes, ma'am."

"Good. Now you try it yourself."

I speared more noodles. The fork felt unfamiliar in this new grasp, but I managed to get them in my mouth without dropping any. I grinned, proud of myself. Lela patted me on the shoulder.

After she taught me how to do something right, she held me to the expectation that I would continue to do it that way. She didn't take any nonsense. If she told me to pick something up and I didn't put it away, she marched me right over there and made me do it while she stood watch. If I didn't eat all my food, she made me sit there until I was finished. Somehow, her not cutting me any slack showed me that she cared.

When I misbehaved, Lela assumed the role of disciplinarian as easily as she played the nurturing caregiver. One of her rules was that I wasn't allowed to go out into the street. I played out in the front yard often, but anything past the sidewalk was off limits. She reminded me every time I walked out the door. One day, I was out in the drive, trying to bounce a basketball. It hit my foot and rolled out into the street. I ran after it without thinking.

"Devin Hughes, get your rear end in the house right now!" Her voice boomed across the yard. She didn't move fast, but that didn't make her less intimidating. I grabbed the ball and high-tailed it to the front door. As soon as my feet hit the entryway, the door slammed behind me, making the floor shake.

"What did I tell you?" she yelled. Her eyes blazed with anger. "Didn't I tell you to stay out of the street? Are you crazy, boy?"

I couldn't think of an answer. I had never seen her like this.

Then she spanked me. It was a quick swat to the backside, and I was shocked but didn't want to cry. Neither of my parents had ever spanked me—physical punishment was a foreign concept to me.

Usually one of my parents picked me up at the front door while Lela waved goodbye. That evening when Dad showed up, Lela waddled down the front steps to walk us to the car. My heart sank into the pit of my stomach.

"I just wanted to let you know that I had to spank Devin today."

Dad looked over at me. "Oh, really? Why is that?"

"While he was playing outside earlier, he chased a ball out into the street without looking. I thought you should hear it from me first."

"I'm glad you did something."

I climbed into the car in silence. Dad walked Lela back to the house and chatted with her for a few minutes. He was quiet as he got in the car. I looked at his face in the rearview mirror. He stared back at me and chuckled.

"Boy, I told you Lela doesn't play around. Bet you won't run out into the street again, huh?" He didn't say anything else, but he had already validated that Lela's reaction was appropriate. Just like touching a hot stove for the first time, I learned to snatch my proverbial hand back; Lela wasn't to be trifled with.

Lela never hit me on my rear again, but she held me accountable if I didn't do what she asked. Her communication style resembled Dad's in some ways: it was straight and real, and she didn't bother with a lot of preamble. She set clear expectations and addressed the heart of the matter.

Although Lela resembled Aunt Fanny physically, the similarities ended there. While Fanny had provided only a roof over Mom's head, Lela became the emotional rock that provided for our family's higher needs. As time went on, she became a surrogate mother to my parents. When they had problems at work or needed some advice, both of them came to pick me up. I played in the other room while they sat around the table with Lela.

Their voices were nothing but a low murmur in the living room, but I could hear their heated tones and feel the tension rolling off them. Little by little, Lela's calm, deliberate voice soothed their agitation. Her oracular presence was instrumental in keeping all three of us on the right track.

When I was five, I stopped going to Lela's. At the time, I didn't know enough to feel any regrets. I had never expected this to last; Dad had told me that Lela was only going to watch me until I was old enough to go to school. This was my first "cinema contract" relationship; I enjoyed it while the story played out, but when the movie was over, I got up and left. She was a part of our lives for more than nine months, but my parents never mentioned her again. Strangely enough, it didn't faze me—I never asked if I would see her again or if we would stay in touch. I simply interacted with whoever showed up on my radar screen and didn't worry about anyone whose blip fell off the field. Through that experience, I learned to focus on the people I had in my life in the moment and not worry about those who drifted away.

In hindsight, of course, it seems strange that my parents never said anything about her; she was the first woman we had a relationship with as a family. Even though she wasn't related, she was the grandmother figure I didn't have, and she was the closest thing I knew to extended family.

CHAPTER 3

STRIKING SPARKS

MY PARENTS SPENT THEIR FIRST FEW YEARS IN DC ISOLATED AND ALONE, with little family and no friends. Their relationship had its ups and downs, and after their initial wave of happiness crested, they argued constantly. My mother crumbled under the stress of two jobs and loneliness. At times, she resented Dad for forcing her to give up the life she would have had in Knoxville: college, sorority life, maybe. Normalcy. Alcohol was a catalyst that set off more than one emotional explosion. Mom had a tongue like a viper. I could hear her screaming through the walls.

I huddled in my bedroom, a sick feeling in my stomach as their voices clashed again and again. Mom's footsteps creaked faster, a surefire sign of the storm to come. The floor shifted under Dad's weight. He tried to avoid the confrontations as much as he could, but Mom eventually boxed him into a corner. I dreaded their fights, but I was only a kid. What could I do? The thud of a body hitting a wall finally drove me out into the living room. Tears poured down my face.

"Stop!" I cried.

They ignored me. Mom stalked Dad as he walked away, pointing her finger in his face as she shrieked.

"Gloria," my dad said. "Gloria, get off me!"

She pushed him at the wall, her hands on his broad shoulders.

"Stop it!" I yelled. I stood paralyzed, dreading what would inevitably come next.

"Gloria, I don't want to hit you!"

My mother got in his face. "You ain't shit, you haven't ever been shit, and you will never be worth anything!"

"Gloria, leave me alone and get out of my face," Dad said.

But she kept pushing, screaming, and provoking him. The sickening crunch of knuckles slamming into bone cut her off mid-sentence. Her head flopped to one side, and time stopped as she fell to the floor. For a moment, the apartment was quiet except for the sound of ragged breathing.

"I told you—"

"You think you're tough?" Mom snapped back into action, pulling to her feet. Angry red marks stood out against her pale skin.

Dad clenched and unclenched his fist. I couldn't take it anymore. "Please, stop!" I grabbed onto Dad's leg and forced myself between them as the battle raged over my head. I tried to push them apart. "Stop it!"

The arguments invariably stopped when I inserted myself. The apartment went quiet, the air thick with pain. Dad lifted me in his arms and sank to the floor with me. Mom slumped against one wall. We were together in our sadness and exhaustion, but separate, with no one making eye contact as we cried. No one apologized. We clung to each other for minutes that seemed like hours. These cease-fires were only temporary, and we all knew it.

After we dispersed, we never spoke about these episodes. I attempted to delete them from my memory as quickly as possible. Still, the problems remained in the apartment with us, festering. Scars were forming.

Toward the end of my time with Lela, my parents' relationship had deteriorated to the point of seeing other people. My mom took me with her when she left my dad the first time. We moved out and into a small apartment. My parents did their best to explain the situation—they just needed some time to work things out. Their words meant nothing to me. I just wanted things the way they had been, but everything was changing too quickly for me to keep up.

Mom started dating a physician she met at work, Harold Smith. I didn't even know he was a doctor at the time; all I knew was that this man would show up and I would stay home with a babysitter—not Lela. I hated seeing Mom with another man. She was so excited to go out and spend time with him that I never felt as if she was present in the moment with me.

Harold Smith was black, had a mustache, wore flashy gold jewelry, and drove a Mercedes. He was articulate and often tried to engage me in games or conversation. I wanted nothing to do with him. I didn't want him in my world, and I could tell it was uncomfortable for my mom and awkward for him. When he talked to me, I just smiled and pretended I needed to do something in my room.

During the day, my mom stuck me in a preschool while she went to work in downtown DC. Outside the classroom that first day, she knelt down to talk to me.

"You're going to have so much fun with all the other kids. You'll see." She seemed nervous, pushing her hair back behind her ears.

Anxiety kept my lips pressed together. I didn't want her to leave me there.

"Come on, Devin. It'll be fun. Don't you think?" She

nodded, trying to prompt the same motion out of me. "Don't you think?"

Please don't leave me, Mom! I wanted to scream, but I gave in and nodded instead.

"I'll be back after work to pick you up, okay?"

I nodded again. She gave me a kiss and wrapped her arms around me in a rare display of maternal affection. I stood frozen, afraid I would do something to ruin the moment. Most of the time, I felt like an inconvenience to Mom; the situation with her and Harold Smith felt wrong, and I never told her how much it hurt to see her going out with him. The moment passed. Mom stood up, smiled at me, and left me stranded in my new environment.

Like the area, this wasn't the United Nations of preschools; this class was 99.9% black. Then there was me, the only kid who looked white. The staff was composed primarily of black women with abrasive personalities. It felt like being dropped in a land where I knew neither the language nor the customs.

The preschool was a big room packed with toys and the noise of a bunch of kids running around unsupervised. I felt isolated and alone in the midst of the chaos spinning around me. The teacher and facilitators didn't instill a lot of order; at least, that was how it seemed to me. I assumed a false bravado, never shedding a tear while I was dying inside.

Dad picked me up from preschool on Fridays, and I spent the weekends with him. The subject of Mom's social life was a constant topic of conversation.

"What's your mom doing these days?"

"Nothing."

"How's pre-school?"

"I don't like it. I don't have any friends."

"Is she going out with somebody?"

"I don't know. She leaves me alone with the babysitter a lot."

"Who's she hanging around with?"

He interrogated me as if I was an accomplice, as if I had "intel" on Mom's activities that I wasn't sharing. I felt torn between them: I wanted to tell my dad, but I didn't want to betray my mom. After a month of confiding about my isolation in pre-school and with the babysitter, Dad finally heard what I was saying. Mom seemed relieved when he offered to take me to live with him.

Spending time with Dad was always fun. I tagged along with him everywhere, even to work at the A&P. He was the supervisor and took great pride in ensuring that all the produce was fresh and looked great. While he worked, I hung out in the back of the produce cooler. Aprons lined the walls. I either lay on the bench and slept or hung out, watching the activity around me, for hours. People came and went, high-fiving me and engaging me until Dad came to check on me with treats from the store. At work with him, I felt insulated from all of the other madness going on in our lives.

Dad rarely let his stresses show around me, but during the separation, I could tell he was tense. He couldn't stand that my mother was dating someone else.

"Do you miss your mom?" he often asked me. I could tell that it was him who desperately missed her.

Several times, Dad took me on stakeouts with him.

We followed my mother in the car, trying not to be seen.

"What are we doing?" I asked.

"Your mom's not in a great place," he said, carefully watching her car. "We're trying to help her out, and one of the ways we can do that is to see what she is doing."

I didn't understand, but I didn't question his reasoning.

When Dad learned who Mom's boyfriend was, we started following him, too. Once, we actually went into Harold Smith's office. The waiting room was tidy, with chairs for patients sprinkled around the room. Magazines lay on end tables, and pictures adorned the walls. There were three people—one elderly and two others around my father's age—sitting in the waiting room when we walked in. I knew this wasn't going to be good. Dad was in one of his weird manic moods.

"I'm here to see Dr. Smith," he said to the women behind the reception desk. His voice was loud and un-regulated, and his eyes glinted.

"Dr. Smith isn't available," one of the women said. She got out of her chair and backed away from Dad.

"I don't care!" Dad shouted. "I need to see him."

I stood in the waiting area, feeling the eyes of all the other patients on us.

The woman still in her chair spoke, her voice soft and calm. "Maybe you can leave a message—"

"Harold Smith!" my dad yelled. "Come out and show your face!"

I wasn't sure whether to stand or sit down. I chose to hover just to the left of my father, near the door. I wanted this nightmare to end.

"You need to leave," the nervous woman said, visibly shaken.

"I'm not going anywhere until I see Dr. Smith!"

"I'll call the police," she said, lifting the phone.

Dad gave her a hard look, and the room was silent. I held my breath, praying the situation wasn't about to get worse.

"Let's go, son," he said finally. I didn't make eye contact with anyone as we walked out the door.

A few days later, Dad woke me in the middle of the night. Outside, in the parking lot, I could see a blaze. Smoke rose toward the dark sky. Our car was on fire.

Dad and I sat helplessly together as we watched our car burn. Neighbors piled out of the building and tried to make small talk with my dad, but he couldn't tear his eyes away from the flames. The fire department showed up, but it was far too late, as the car was charred to a crisp.

"Are you the owner of the vehicle?"

Dad nodded.

"We have some questions for you, if you'd like to file a report."

"I have to put my son to bed," Dad muttered. He grabbed me by the hand and dragged me back inside.

"It was Harold Smith," Dad said to me. He had no proof, but he was utterly convinced it was the doctor. I couldn't understand why someone would burn our car. Though I was anxious and stressed by the event, I was with my father and felt comfort in that.

The car was removed the next day, but the evidence of the fire remained until the parking lot was repaved more than a year later. Until he was able to buy a new car, we rode a bike to his work. I was so small that I sat on the handlebars while he held me and pedaled hard. The trip had to be three or four miles, and it was freezing cold. He pumped us up and down hills, laughing his butt off at my squeals of excitement. In spite of the chaos that had brought us to that point, this stands out as a great memory for me: the two of us surviving tough times together. He made do with what he had, and he made it fun. He did his best to filter out the stress my mother's relationship caused him, instead focusing on what he could teach me.

"You can either find a way or an excuse," he said. "We find a way. We survive."

I nodded as the frigid air whipped my face.

"What's your last name?" he asked.

"Hughes."

"What's that? I didn't hear you."

"Hughes!" I exclaimed.

"That's right—Hughes. Your name is Hughes, and we get it done."

Every day on the bike was another pep talk, another bolstering of my self-esteem.

"People fall," he said over the wind and traffic. "They get hurt, but you got to get up. Tough times don't last," he added. "Tough people do."

My father passed on some valuable life lessons in unobtrusive ways. Simply by keeping a positive attitude around me, he transferred constant instructions for survival and coping strategies. As part of his nurturing way as a father, he instilled in me the habit of self-talk—reasoning, soothing affirmations to help keep calm within realistic perspective. He used self-talk to calm down his internal physical system and, accordingly, his thoughts. He fueled me with constant pep talks to keep my self-esteem bolstered, so I wouldn't get down and depressed.

The phrase he repeated to me most often was, "I am, I can, I will. I am, I can, I will." Any time I came to a place in my life where I doubted my ability or lacked confidence, I repeated those words to myself: "I am, I can, I will. I *am* somebody, I *can* do it, I *will* do it." Through repetition, I learned to cope and move forward almost unconsciously. I'm not sure he realized at the time that he was teaching me the habit of self-talk, but every time I think of those words, I picture the two of us on Dad's bicycle, riding to work and making the best of the burned-up car situation.

Another part of the equation in keeping my spirits up during tough times was to turn everything into a fun learning experience. I wanted to get out and go places, but all we had was the bike, so Dad turned learning how to ride the bus into an adventure. He picked out interesting destinations and events, and we took the bus to go see the monuments and museums in the city, or we went to sporting events. The overall message was that I should never be dependent on one thing. My parents were separated, my mom was dating someone else, and we didn't have a car—or much else, for that matter—but he kept us busy so that I didn't have time to dwell on the negative. His constant stream of positivity created a feeling of security for me that I didn't feel with my mother.

This cycle—stakeout, bike, daily life, stakeout—continued for months until Harold Smith confronted my father on one of our "outings." By this time, we finally had a new vehicle. We were idling outside Harold Smith's dry cleaner when he walked up to our car window.

"Clarkie, what is going on?" he asked, leaning in. "Is it a coincidence that you happen to be at all the same locations I'm at?"

"No," Dad said, calm and direct. "I just want to see the man who is breaking up our family."

"I'm not breaking up your family," Harold Smith said. "That's your wife's decision. She wasn't happy."

"Don't give me that bullshit!" Dad snapped. "*You're* doing it, and I just have something to show you here."

He pointed to the pistol that lay on the front seat between us. Nervous and excited, I watched as the expression on Harold Smith's face turned to fear and shock. The stare they were locked in seemed like one between two gunslingers.

"I just want to make sure you understand that I'm not playing," Dad said.

No more words were exchanged. The doctor looked at him, at me, and at the gun, and did an abrupt about-face from the car. He started lightly jogging toward his car, and my dad stared him down. He remained parked until Harold Smith drove away. It was a surreal moment for me.

"Son," Dad said, "if you believe in something enough, you have to stand for it."

"Were you really going to shoot him?" I asked in disbelief as we left the parking lot.

"No, son, I wasn't going to shoot him," Dad said. "I was hoping he wouldn't put me in a bad position, but sometimes in this world, you got to bluff. I was willing to go right to the edge, but I wasn't going to shoot anybody."

My adrenaline was still rushing when Dad added jovially, "I'm not crazy, boy! I'm not going back to jail."

Just like that, he diffused the situation and turned it into a joke. This was similar to how he'd built his reputation in prison, when he had to bluff as if he was a tough, crazy badass. He put on these masks and dared you to get closer, and when the situation was over, he went on as though it had never happened.

Shortly after that incident, the doctor broke off the relationship with my mother, and my parents reunited. Their relationship remained tumultuous, however … and my mother brought home a bad habit. I was too young to articulate the effect the drugs had on her; I picked up on the cues, but didn't know how to interpret them. I was just happy to have her back. I craved any semblance of stability I could get.

Even with all three of us together again, my father was the primary cook in our house. We ate what he had eaten as a kid, and my diet consisted exclusively of soul food. Breakfast was eggs, grits, and some kind of meat, typically scrapple or bacon. Scrapple is all the scraps from a hog mashed together. I loved putting it in a bowl with my eggs and grits. When our usual breakfast wasn't available, I ate Cream of Wheat. To me, pancakes, French toast, and waffles were what rich white people ate. Dinner consisted of more soul food; we ate collard greens, cornbread, rice, black-eyed peas, catfish, macaroni and cheese, and pretty much every part of the hog, including pigs' feet and ham hocks. Steak was a huge treat that I looked forward to with great anticipation.

We were living in Silver Spring, Maryland at the time, and I was back in a home daycare program while my parents worked. This daycare was a much better environment than the nursery school my mom had taken me to. The woman who ran the daycare had a few children I could play with. There was an alley right behind their apartment, and I will never forget the day I threw a ball back there. Walking deep into the alley to retrieve it, I saw a man slouched in the corner with his head cocked to one side. The ball had rolled within twenty feet of him. Nervous around strangers, I was torn between not wanting to go near him and wanting to get the ball. I eased up but stayed ready to run like hell if this crazy cracker stood up. As I came closer, the guy started to look like some freakazoid monster; he wasn't moving at all. Then I saw that he had blood all down the side of his face and body. Someone had put a bullet in his head.

I ran back to the house, where the babysitter was watching TV and kids were playing like any other day.

"There's a man down in the corner of the alley!" I said. "He's laying all weird with blood on his head and a funny look on his face." I was breathless but calm; I was not new to odd situations.

At first she didn't believe me. Then kids began running outside to see, and she followed. She screamed when she saw the man, and we kids stared at him as if he were a science experiment.

"Get back into the apartment!" she told us all. "Come on, let's go!"

She herded us back inside and called the police.

When my parents got there, I told them what had happened, but they didn't spend a whole lot of time on it. Neither did I. Seeing the dead man didn't make me think of life or death. I thought of it as a freak show, as if the man were a Martian. I couldn't help but wonder what had happened, but I figured that whatever it was, it was. My parents seemed to agree.

"Hey, sometimes there are bad people in the world," Dad said. "Who knows what happened to him. You just got to be careful." That was that.

In some ways, my life was very much like walking across a minefield. I had no idea where or when the mines would blow, but invariably someone would step on them. I just did my best not to be that unlucky bastard. That was how I was learning to view the world.

CHAPTER 4

ANODYNE

ALTHOUGH MY MOTHER WAS PHYSICALLY BACK WITH US, IT FELT AS IF WE HAD A STRANGER IN OUR HOME.

Before, she had always seemed on a mission to catch up to some invisible force, running a constant chase in which she never reached her goal. Though this meant she rarely seemed present in the moment with me, at least she had energy; she was vivacious. After splitting with the doctor, that outgoing personality had been replaced by a drug addiction that turned her into the living dead.

Substance abuse wasn't new to me. My father was already a borderline alcoholic. He drank beer from time to time but mostly hard liquor. To me, it was all whiskey. He wasn't a sloppy drunk, but I could tell when he was intoxicated because he laughed nonstop. At first I didn't appreciate it, but it's funny what you come to normalize when you are submerged in it on a daily basis.

Both my parents were functional addicts. They each worked two jobs to support their habits and our family. At the time, five hundred dollars a week was a lot of money, and they each made at least that. Combined, they brought in over sixty thousand dollars a year. With both of them working so many hours and only support-ing one child, we should have been able to live in a real house. I was no Sherlock Holmes, but I picked up on patterns of behavior that explained what happened to all that money.

"I'm going out." Mom's voice carried to my bedroom from the living room. It was late, past ten, and I heard her shuffle through the clutter on the dining room table. "Where are my keys?"

I dragged myself out of bed, yawning. "Where are you going?"

"I just have to run an errand downtown," she lied. It was the second time this week that she was leaving me at home after dark.

"But it's late."

"I have to pick up something from somebody at work." She swept a pile of papers to the side and found her keys. "Be good. I'll be home soon."

In addition to my mother's regular "errands," drug language was a staple part of my daily vocabulary; "lovely" was a term I heard often. It was marijuana sprinkled with PCP.

"Devin," my mother called from her spot on the beat-up sofa. It was Friday night, and Dad sat with her, laughing his silly, intoxicated laugh. Mom's eyes were glazed in the sad, zombie-like stare I saw her in most often. She picked at a hole in the slipcover that hid much bigger tears.

"Don't do drugs," she said. "They're bad. Drugs are bad." She looked exhausted, with deep bags under her green eyes.

I shuffled across the living room. Even through my socks, I could feel the dirt in the carpet. The stench of week-old kitty litter mingled with the sweet, ashy smell of pot smoke. She hadn't done any housework in weeks; she spent most of her time at home sleeping between shifts.

Living with the cluttered dining room table, grimy bathrooms, and the permanent disaster zone of our kitchen, I had already deduced that drugs were bad.

Besides the embarrassing state of the apartment, drugs kept us from prospering. The only thing besides drugs and alcohol my parents spent significant money on was a nice car now and then. It was ghetto philosophy, to project an image of affluence that didn't exist.

"Drugs mess with your mind," Dad reinforced. "They'll take you off the yellow brick road." He had been recently diagnosed as manic-depressive. The drugs exacerbated the highs, causing explosive shifts in his mood and behavior. He would go days without sleeping and spent countless hours away from the apartment. His clothes reflected his loud, edgy personality during those highs. The bright red Washington Redskins cowboy hat perched on his head was a sure-fire way to draw gawks from strangers. Neither Mom nor I knew where he went during those highs. Often he'd come home with the soles of his feet scraped and bleeding because he'd been jogging through the city streets barefoot.

When his mood swung to the other end of the spectrum, Dad started fights. The shortage of money sparked more than one firestorm.

"I just got paid last week, Gloria!" Dad yelled from the living room.

"And?" Mom shot back. "What's your point?"

I closed my bedroom door and tried to ignore them. They were like a scratched record, doomed to repeat the same song.

"I'm sick of all the money going up in smoke!" Dad's voice carried through the thin walls as he stomped and swore all the way down the hall. The front door slammed as he left.

Marijuana baggies, bongs, and other drug paraphernalia littered the apartment. I never saw my parents getting high, but I wasn't naïve. The distinctive sound of
water gurgling through a bong behind the bedroom door
became a soundtrack to my daily life. When my parents were gone, I snuck into their room to investigate
the bongs. One of them was giant—eighteen inches of
thick, cloudy glass with a metal mouthpiece. Dirty water
pooled in the bottom of the bowl. It sloshed from side to
side as I picked it up and turned it in my hands. A sick,
horrible smell emanated from inside. Curious, I stuck my
index finger into the mouthpiece and felt around. Gritty
particles that felt like sand clung to the tip of my finger.
Some of the bigger pieces were actual marijuana seeds.
I studied the bongs for hours, trying to piece together
the mystery of why my parents spent so much of their
time and energy on drugs.

Since my parents were always working, I spent a lot
of time isolated and alone in our apartment. When they
were around, though, both of them worked hard on my
self-esteem.

"You're special," Mom told me. "Unique. The best of
both worlds."

As a realist, my father also prepared me for a world
I wouldn't fit into. He said, "Some people won't accept
you, but that's okay. They never accept the great ones."

Kids grow up in their own little bubbles. Each is
constructed differently, and for the first few years of life,
most are happy with what they have. Until a certain
point, most are unable to compare their lot to that of
their peers. That's not to say that, out at the park, one

child isn't envious of another's toy truck or shovel, but most don't look around at the age of three or four thinking they're missing out on something. The same was true for me. Despite the chaos with my parents, I was largely happy with my life until it hit me that I was completely different from most of the other kids.

My dad drove me to school on the first day of kindergarten in 1974. I was already intimidated and anxious about whether I would fit in, but I was not prepared for what awaited me.

The buzz of excited chatter fell silent when we walked in the door, and the flurry of motion between rows of small desks came to an abrupt stop. Whispers flew back and forth as the kids craned their necks to get a good look at us—this large black man holding the hand of a small Caucasian-looking boy.

"Who is that?"

"What's that little white kid doing with a black man?"

"Quiet down," the teacher shushed the other children, but the look in her eyes echoed their questions. A slight wrinkle creased the bridge of her nose as she pointed at an open seat.

The awkwardness I already felt because I looked nothing like my father amplified as everyone sized us up. Now it wasn't just an internalized feeling of strangeness—now our physical incongruence was something that literally set me apart from the other children. It would have been different if the atmosphere in the room was one of curiosity, but the air was thick with judgment. Beyond the initial shocked stares, my classmates and teacher let their eyes slide past me without really looking. There was no engagement; they treated me with a passive-aggressive type of racism, rejecting me based solely on external criteria. A mixture of sadness and insecurity tightened my chest as I took my seat. I didn't know it then, but those feelings would soon become my constant, if silent, companions.

CHAPTER 5

SEVERED ROOTS

WHEN I WAS GROWING UP, I KNEW THAT MY MOM HAD LEFT HOME AS A TEENAGER, but my parents didn't talk about it; all I knew was that neither had a relationship with their parents. I was eight years old the first time I had the opportunity to learn more about my family; my mom was sending me to Tennessee to meet my grandparents.

"Hurry up, we're going to be late getting to the airport," Mom called from the kitchen.

I dragged my overstuffed bag out of my room. "Why do I have to go by myself?"

"I don't see why anybody's going to see that redneck cracker at all," Dad chimed in from the couch. Those were the first words he'd spoken all morning. He refused to come to the airport with us. "That man is everything that is wrong with the South."

"He is their only grandchild. They have a right to meet him," Mom said. Her voice was more guilty than passionate, as though she were trying to make amends for cutting the emotional umbilical cord with her family.

The new polyester sofa cover rustled as Dad swung his legs over the side and sat up. He pulled me to his side. "Son, do you remember what I told you?"

"Yeah, Dad."

"Who can you trust?"

"Nobody."

"Nobody is right. You can trust me, your mom, and the man in the mirror, but that's it."

Mom opened the door. "Out. We're leaving."

I dragged my feet across the living room.

Dad called after me. "Don't you trust that ignorant

cracker, Devin. Not for a minute. He hates all black people."

"Now," Mom said, and pointed out the door.

Dad crossed his arms and lay back on the couch, resuming his silent protest.

At the airport, Mom walked me through the chaotic airport hustle to the gate. She hugged me. "I love you," she said.

When the flight started boarding, an airline attendant came and took my hand. I waved to Mom before walking up the ramp with the attendant. Mom waved back, a sad look on her face. Even though it was her idea that I should meet my grandparents, she wouldn't come with me. In her mind, she had walked away from Tennessee and started a brand new life. She was like a mafia donna who had gone into the witness protection program, changed her identity, and caught amnesia along the way.

In some ways the flight felt like it would never end; in others it didn't feel long enough. One part of me was excited to see the new land we were flying toward, like Indiana Jones searching for new civilizations. A much larger part was nervous; my parents had fled for a *reason*, after all. Dad had never said anything disparaging about my grandmother, so I wasn't afraid to meet her, but the picture my father painted of my grandfather was unnerving. As the plane touched down on the tarmac in Knoxville, I felt as if I were landing behind enemy lines, with the heavy pack of my father's distrust strapped to my back and no weapon to rely on but my own wits.

Until now, my contact with white people had been

extremely limited. The only interaction I had with Caucasian people was with kids on school sports teams, and I had never encountered one that could be considered a hillbilly. Now, every step off the plane brought me closer to the man my father considered the symbol of racist hate.

I took a deep breath and kept my guard up as I scanned the small crowd at the arrival gate. Two white women in loud, flowery dresses waved at me eagerly. I froze. Was I supposed to hug them? They were strangers to me.

"Well, I never," the older one said. "It's lovely to meet you, Devin." She reached toward me, hesitation in her movements. After a moment she put her hands on my shoulders. "I'm your grandma, and this is your Aunt Beverly."

"You're so tall!" Beverly said with a smile as she ruffled my hair. "You didn't look so tall in the pictures Gloria sent."

I let myself smile a little. This wasn't so bad. If Mom had sent them pictures, she must still care about these people. They were country, with their out-of-date clothes and strong accents, but they seemed genuine. Apprehension turned to curiosity as I eased my guard. Why would my mother send them pictures of me but never show me photos of them?

I followed them out to the parking lot, my father's warnings ringing in my head. I kept my eyes open and my mouth shut, resolved to be alert and keep my defenses strong. Still, I couldn't help staring out the windows at this strange new world. For an inner-city kid, the undeveloped land we passed was a culture shock in itself. My face was so close to the window that my nose left a little cloudy smudge.

"Here we are!" my grandmother said, turning off the main road.

Hills of grass and farmland framed a long driveway between the road and my grandparents' ranch house. Gravel crunched under the tires and rattled against the bottom of the car as we passed a pigpen and chicken coop teeming with animals. The first thing I noticed when we approached the house was a brand new basketball hoop towering next to the carport. I started to feel hope. My grandmother must have put that up especially for me; after all, there were no other kids around that I knew of. Maybe these people weren't as bad as Dad said they were. My grandmother killed the engine.

"Home sweet home, honey!" she said cheerily.

We climbed out of the car. A collie ran up to meet me, tail wagging furiously as its tongue flapped out of its mouth. I laughed, patting its smooth head, and the dog jumped up and licked my face.

"That's Molly," Aunt Beverly told me. "Looks like you two are going to be great friends."

"Devin, let's get your bag out of the car and I'll show you where … " Grandma's voice trailed off as her husband came around the corner from the back of the house.

At six foot four and over two hundred pounds, my grandfather loomed over me. His arms ended in giant, meaty Paul Bunyan hands that looked as if they could grab me by the neck and choke the life out me. Every horrible thing Dad had said about this man came rushing back at me. We eyed each other; I could tell he didn't know what to do, and I didn't know what to say.

He spit a long strand of tobacco juice on the ground between us. "Well," he said, breaking the tense silence. "Looks like we got us a city boy down here on the farm." His accent was straight out of *The Dukes of Hazzard*. I barely understood him. Unlike my grandmother, his face was neither friendly nor welcoming.

I stared up at him. Molly jumped by my side, but I ignored her. I felt as if I finally understood what my father had been saying all these years. I didn't trust the look of this man standing over me.

"Oh, you leave him alone," Grandma said. "He just got off a plane."

Her words made the awkwardness go away temporarily, like a cold treated with cough syrup.

"Come on, Devin. Let's go find your bedroom."

I gave my grandfather a wide berth as I followed my grandmother toward the front door. I glanced at him over my shoulder, not wanting to let him out of my sight. The skin on the back of his neck was red from the sun. That must be why Dad always called him a redneck!

Once inside the house, I started to wonder if I really had stepped onto another planet. My grandmother kept an immaculate home. White, tidy, and quiet, it was the polar opposite of our filthy apartment in Silver Spring, Maryland. Although I felt reasonably comfortable in my hood, hanging with my black friends, the color of my skin was a constant reminder of my difference from everyone around me. I was never black enough to fit into my own world. Here, I was in a parallel universe where

I was not white enough to fit in with my mother's family. Would that paradox continue to haunt me for the rest of my life?

The contrast between this world and the one I knew made me want to learn more about my mom and how she had grown up in this house. What had she been like as a kid? Why was it so impossible for Grandma and Grandpa to accept my father? Those were questions I didn't know how to ask. Ignoring them seemed best for everyone involved.

There were no other kids for me to play with, so I spent hours shooting hoops outside or playing with the dog. When I was tired or it was too hot out, I roamed the house, careful to stay out of my grandfather's way. Family pictures covered the walls, and I searched them for clues as to what my mom had been like before she met my dad.

In these photos, my mother was a vibrant, smiling teenager. I hardly recognized this thin, healthy young woman whose green eyes looked like mine. In one photo taken on the farm with her sister, she seemed so present in the moment that I sat there and stared for what seemed like hours, trying to connect the dots between her and the exhausted woman I knew, whose only joy came from cigarettes, Coca Cola, and food. I couldn't help but wonder if my grandparents had put these photos up just because I was coming, or if they maybe did still care about my mother. I felt as if I was learning my history by accident.

After spending some time with my grandmother, I couldn't quite believe she was my mother's mother.

She was pale white, with dyed blond hair and an accent that could slice a dinner role. She was slim and walked quickly, smiling often and for no apparent reason. I caught myself staring at her, looking for signs that this woman was actually my mom's mom. Despite the incongruities, it made no sense to me why my mother would give up everything to run off with a much older, married black man. My mother's heart was a mystery to me. So, for that matter, was my grandfather's.

I cannot recall ever having a serious conversation with him. I sensed that he was uncomfortable around me; in his mind, I was the byproduct of an unholy union. I, meanwhile, had obviously heard nothing good about white men in the South—they were "rednecks," "crackers," and "bigots," and he fit the profile. I avoided him as much as possible for fear of him hurting me, though I had nothing to base my anxiety on except Dad's voice in the back of my head.

Nights were tense. I lay awake in bed, listening for the creak of floorboards under his shifting weight. He moved with a slow, lumbering shuffle in the daytime. By moonlight, he was my own personal version of the bogeyman. Every noise outside my bedroom door made me jump. I fought sleep as long as I could; when I closed my eyes, I imagined him stealing through the shadows, reaching for me with those lumberjack hands. I stayed up late every night, waiting for the sweet silence after my grandparents' bedroom door shut. Only then could I close my eyes. It was a bizarre feeling for an eight-year-old, but already I carried such baggage from my parents about my grandparents and white people in general that it was hard to comfortably share the same space as them.

Mealtimes were the highlights of staying with my grandparents. The three of us sat down to a home-cooked meal every night: eggs, grits, tomatoes, and freshly squeezed orange juice. The country staples were a far cry from the soul food I was accustomed to back home. I sat beside my grandmother, never taking my wary eyes off Grandpa.

"So, how is your mother doing?" Grandma asked as she piled food on my plate.

"She's fine."

"That's good. Pass the milk down here." That was the extent of the conversation about my mother.

Dinner was quiet and awkward. For dessert, we had some of Grandma's frozen fruit. She froze everything, but my favorites were the peaches. While we ate, Grandpa cleared his throat and finally broke his silence.

His eyes narrowed as he studied me. "How's your nigger dad doing?"

I startled but tried not to show it. "He's good. He works hard."

"Do people stare at you when you go out with him?"

I didn't answer right away. At first I thought he was trying to elicit some sort of reaction from me. Over time, I came to see that this was just a part of the way he looked at the world.

"Not really," I lied.

"Does it make you nervous to go out with him?"

"No, everything is just fine. We don't ever have problems." Grandpa wasn't on our team. I didn't want to give him any indication that we were vulnerable.

After dinner, I gathered the leftovers and placed them on an aluminum pan. Then I got to run the scraps down to the pigpen at the bottom of the hill. I watched the feeding frenzy with delight. Before walking back up the hill, counting the hours to the next meal so I could do it again. The smell of dirt, sweat, pigs, and farm was thrilling to me, and so very different from my apartment back home.

All of the contrast I experienced between my grandparents' world and my life with my parents made me start reevaluating my own beliefs. Until now, I had taken everything my father told me about the South and my mother's family as gospel truth. It was as though he'd put food in my mouth, and I had carried it under my tongue to Knoxville. Only when I saw what these people lived like did I start to chew. The taste was slightly different than my father's description.

I only visited my grandparents for two summers. Between visits, my parents talked about them in past tense—there was no acknowledgment of a current relationship. There were no Christmas cards, no phone calls, no family reunions, no connection at all. I relished the chance to step into my parents' past and try to figure out where I came from, but when they found out that Grandpa referred to Dad as a nigger and me as a half-breed, they never let me go back. That was the end of my relationship with my mother's parents. It was time to move on.

CHAPTER 6

THE SEEDS
OF SUCCESS

ISOLATION TAUGHT ME SELF-RELIANCE. I was a latchkey kid, so I spent a lot of time alone while my parents were at work. After school, I came straight home, didn't talk to strangers, and made sure no one followed me. At home, there wasn't anyone home to greet me or hug me or get me something to drink; anything I wanted, I had to get for myself. If I needed something to eat, I grabbed cereal or made a sandwich. The routine demanded that I call one of my parents to let them know I was safe, and then I planted myself in front of the TV for a few hours. Shows with black central characters, like *The Jeffersons* and *Good Times*, were my favorites. Alone in that apartment, I lived vicariously through the humorous dysfunction of TV characters, soaking up their body language, interactions, and jokes.

As I grew older, I tried to spend as little time inside our apartment as I could, especially when my parents were home. Being outdoors was a refuge from the constant gurgle of bongs and my parents' regular screaming matches. Dad liked escaping the tension, too. If he wasn't working, he came out with me.

Dad stepped into my room on a Saturday morning. "Grab your bat and glove. Let's go." In one hand he held a five-gallon bucket of beat-up balls.

I jumped up, grabbed my gear, and raced out of my room. Dad stood by the entry hallway, tying his shoes. Mom had gotten home from the late shift a few hours earlier. She sat on the couch in front of the TV, a blank expression on her face.

"Where are you going?" she asked listlessly.

"Dad's taking me out to play baseball," I said, hopping

on one foot as I pulled on my sneakers.

She stared past me at the TV and didn't respond. Even though they were technically together, my parents seemed to exist in two separate worlds.

"Okay, bye!" I shouted and ran past Dad and into the hallway. I let one hand trail across the wall as my feet thumped down the hall. The apartment door banged shut somewhere behind me. Once I stood outside in the sunshine, I stopped and waited for Dad to catch up.

"Do you want to practice batting today or should we just go to the elementary school and throw the ball back and forth?" he asked.

"I want to bat, too."

"Then let's head over to the high school."

We walked together, the bucket of baseballs swinging between us.

"You remember what I told you last time?"

I swung my bat in a big circle to loosen up my arm. "Elbows down, eye on the ball, swing for the fences?"

Dad smiled. "Let's see if you can hit it all the way into the outfield this time. You know, if you can believe it—"

"I can achieve it!" I finished for him.

At the field, we saw a few other kids that I knew. I wasn't the only one who would rather run around outside than sit at home—when we were at the field, we lived through the major leaguers. My dad knew all the neighborhood kids, too, and he waved to them as we passed.

Dad walked out to the pitcher's mound and I stepped up to the plate. He had been lugging around at least thirty baseballs in that plastic pail, and one by one, he threw them all, giving me pointers or encouragement after every swing. When all the balls lay scattered in the grass, we ran through the outfield together, picked them all up, and started over.

"Okay, Devin, now what?" he asked when his arm got tired.

"Pitching!"

"All right, you going to bring the heat?"

"I got the heat."

We stood under the early spring sun tossing that ball back and forth with no regard for time. The ball cracked against the palm of my glove, adding a steady backbeat to our conversations.

"You ready for this?" I called. I stuck my nose inside the collar of my T-shirt and wiped the sweat off my forehead.

"I'm ready," Dad shouted back. "Show me what you've got."

I stood straight and held my glove up to my face. It smelled of dried sweat and old leather. The ball spun through my fingers as I adjusted my grip. I set up the pitch and let it fly.

"Whoo-ee!" Dad yelled. "That's hot! Hot, hot, hot!" He tossed the ball from hand to hand. "With that arm I should call the major leagues right now!"

"Yeah, right." I rolled my eyes but couldn't help grinning.

He tossed the ball back. "You know, son, you can be anything you want. That's how important confidence is."

I didn't answer. I threw the ball harder.

"I'm serious. You should never doubt yourself."

In a way, our time together was an outlet for him as well. It allowed him to step away from some of the realities of his world. I never really connected the dots between my father's words and his own actions; he spent a lot of time convincing me that I could do anything I wanted to, if I only put my mind to it, but he didn't practice what he preached.

After a while, some of the other kids joined us and we all threw the ball around.

"Hey, did you see *The Bad News Bears*?" one of the guys asked. "How cool would it be if we had a team like that?"

We'd been practicing for hours. I was tired, and Dad was exhausted.

"That's enough for today," he said. Sweat stained the neck and armpits of his T-shirt. "Let's go to the 7-Eleven and grab a Slurpee. What do you say?"

"Yeah!" A Slurpee was the best treat to round out a perfect day.

"You know what?" Dad said as we walked to the store. "We're going to start a team."

"A team? What do you mean?"

"A local team. I'm going to be the coach."

"No way!" I couldn't believe it. I had never been part of a real *team* before.

The next week, he went to the local community association—and that was the beginning of the Tigers. I recruited kids I knew and liked from the neighborhood, and used my spirit of influence to persuade other kids from school who I thought were good athletes. Like me, none of them had played organized sports before, and we were thrilled.

The whole process made me indescribably happy. I felt possessed by the spirit of baseball; I looked forward to practice through the entire school day. At lunch, I joked with my teammates. Every day someone would brag, "I'm going to strike you out," or "I'm going to hit a home run." We were competitive, even though most of us had never played an actual game of baseball, and we didn't know the finer points of fielding the ball.

Dad knew baseball and he knew kids, and—like any great coach—he could relate to us in meaningful ways. Some of the players didn't have fathers at home, so he became their surrogate dad. It was a great opportunity for me to spend time with him and see him affect others in a positive way. Everything we did, Dad turned into a competition. He kept up a constant play-by-play in his upbeat, positive way that resonated with all the guys on the team. He coached from the pitcher's mound and rotated his players through the outfield.

"Batter up!" he shouted.

Timmy, one of the kids who'd never played baseball before, walked up to the plate. The bat shook a little in his grip.

"All right, nice and easy," Dad said. "Just keep your eyes on the ball and swing."

"You got this, Timmy!" we shouted from the outfield, pounding our fists in our gloves.

The ball got away from Dad as he let go … and it flew straight for Timmy's head. Timmy didn't move; he didn't know how to react, or that he could duck.

The ball cracked against the side of his batting helmet. Timmy's face reddened and he looked confused; I could tell he wanted to cry. We all looked at each other. Then came Dad's unmistakable, contagious chuckle. His whole body shook as the chuckle grew into loud, high-pitched laughter. There was no meanness in it; it was all about being present in the moment, not taking mistakes too seriously. One by one, we all joined in the laughter. The hilarity grew as Dad fell on the ground, wiping tears from his eyes.

"All right, guys," Dad said once he'd gotten control of himself. "Come in here."

We all gathered around him. Timmy was still red-faced but smiling.

"It'll be okay," Dad told Timmy. He clapped Timmy's small shoulder with his own large hand. "Keep your chin up. Next time you see a ball coming at your head, make sure you duck, knucklehead."

That moment stuck with me. Dad made us see that it was okay to fail, so long as we tried. He never embarrassed a kid who already felt self-conscious. When he sent us out to run bases, he pulled Timmy aside and gave him a few pointers in private.

Playing baseball built my self-confidence. We had a great team; while we all wanted to be great individually, we all wanted one another to win, too. I could play any position on the field, and I was one of the two top Tigers. Dad encouraged me all along the way.

"Game time, Devin. Let's go," Dad shouted on his way out the door one day.

I threw on my cap and grabbed my mitt. For a moment

I considered going to say good-bye to Mom, but when her door was closed, she usually wanted to be left alone. I pressed my ear to the door and listened. The familiar gurgling sound was muffled, but it was there. Without a word, I raced out to meet Dad at the car.

The Buick gleamed in the afternoon sun. Six other players stood next to it, shoving each other away from the doors and laughing. None of the parents of the other boys in the neighborhood went to games, so Dad drove us all.

"Pile in, guys," he said, sliding behind the wheel.

More pushing and shoving as we scrambled into the backseat, seven deep, shouting about how many home runs we were all going to hit. Even if there had been enough seatbelts for all of us, we wouldn't have been able to fasten them. We laughed nonstop as we caravanned our way to the field. Some of the guys brought straws along, and we pegged other cars with a barrage of spitball sniper-fire from the back seat. Hanging out with the other kids on the team provided a sense of community that I saw on TV but hadn't, until now, experienced firsthand.

We had a team of thirteen players, all of us instilled with a sense of cockiness and bravado, thanks to my dad. We felt connected to something bigger than ourselves, and we went all the way to the championship that first year. Jerry, one of my good buddies, pitched our last game. I played shortstop. In the bottom of the ninth, Phillip, the biggest kid on the opposing team, stepped up to the plate. We were up by two runs; we could taste our victory already. Dad jogged out to the pitcher's mound. I ran in to meet them.

"Jerry," he said, "I know you're going to want to strike him out, but keep it low and away. If you put it in his eyes, he is going to kill it. Got it?"

Jerry nodded, but his eyes glinted. He wanted to do what he wanted to do.

Dad walked back to the dugout. Jerry stood straight and tall. He drew back his arm, raised his leg for balance, and burned a fastball right down the middle of the plate.

Phillip crushed it.

I stood, craning my neck, and watched the ball sail way over my head. The left fielder scrambled to reach it. Phillip made it to third base before we were able to bring the ball back to the infield. We lost by one run.

The Tigers were devastated. We couldn't believe it. Back in the dugout we were all in tears. Every head on the bench hung low, but Jerry took the loss personally. His shoulders shook as he cried.

"Now, come on, guys," Dad said to us. "You all came so far. This was an opportunity to learn, and this time it wasn't meant to be. We'll be back. You will be champions."

Dad knew that Jerry had dropped the ball right down the middle without listening to his advice, but he didn't chastise him in front of the team. Instead, he took him aside and talked to him privately. I never found out what he said to him.

Watching my father coach the Tigers reinforced a lot of the behaviors that I valued in him; he was fun, energetic, a great teacher, and he embodied the power of a positive attitude. For me, sports became associated with the mentality that I could do anything I wanted to do. My self-esteem blossomed. I loved being part of a team, and I wanted more of it—it was like vitamins for me.

I had been playing pickup basketball as long as I could dribble a ball, but baseball was the catalyst that launched my love of organized sports. The structure and consistency was so different from what I knew at home. I talked about sports nonstop to anyone who would listen. Even Mom couldn't tune me out completely. Through a friend at the doctor's office where she worked, she had gotten a flyer for an overnight basketball camp run by Wes Unseld. Wes Unseld was an NBA Hall of Famer who played for the Washington Bullets; everyone knew about him. Five days out of the apartment sounded like heaven, and playing basketball every day under Wes Unseld was just icing on the cake. I begged to go. My parents said yes.

I was jittery with nervous energy as my dad slowed the car to a stop in front of the college campus where camp was held. Everywhere I looked, I saw parents, cars, counselors, and kids bustling around in loosely controlled chaos.

Dad turned around in the driver's seat. "I want you to get up there, I want you to hustle, and I want you to work hard. If you work hard, you will keep getting better."

"I know, Dad."

Mom stared out the window at the parents saying good-bye. I opened the door and stepped out onto the sidewalk. Dad grabbed my bag for me and put his hand on my shoulder. "It's okay to be nervous."

"I'm not nervous," I lied.

"This is going to be a great experience."

I tried not to stare at some of the kids who were crying as their parents drove away.

"This is a great opportunity. You said you wanted to get better, and you're going to get to meet Wes. He's supposed to be pretty involved in the camp."

I took a big breath, putting on a strong face. "Okay, Dad. See you guys in a few days."

We said good-bye and I found my way to my room in the dorms. Kids were everywhere, all of us drawn together by our love for basketball and our desire to improve our game. There were some kids from my neck of the woods, but there were others from all different social and economic backgrounds. You could tell by looking at their shoes that they had a very different upbringing. I wore a pair of Pumas; they weren't the latest and greatest, but they were decent. My practice clothes consisted of some beat-up shorts and T-shirts. Some of the other kids had color-coordinated uniforms and basketball shoes I'd only seen on TV commercials. Invariably, the kids with the nicest gear were white.

As usual, I gravitated toward the black kids. I didn't have any white friends in my neighborhood or at school; I felt uncomfortable around them, and my neighborhood friends felt the same way. We saw the white kids in the school cafeteria with their packed lunches, and I thought how nice it would be, just once, to have the luxury of someone taking the time to pack my lunch. I imagined these kids sitting at breakfast tables with their parents, eating fluffy pancakes smothered in maple syrup, maybe with some fruit in them. Pancakes were rich white people food to me. It wasn't until I was much older that I realized you could buy a box for ninety-nine cents, throw some water in the mix, and be done. Back then, the *idea* of pancakes was as unreachable to me as these kids' vacations. I'd overhear that they were going on ski trips, and I would go to the library and look up skiing because I had no idea what that was. In my mind, packed lunches and vacations weren't a class thing; they were a race thing, and for all intents and purposes, I was black.

Of course, to those who didn't already know me, I needed to show my street credibility. I needed to let people know that I, like most black kids, looked down on white kids who had no understanding of the issues and drama that went with our culture. I needed to prove I wasn't one of them. The way I fit in was by cracking on everybody; I was sarcastic and witty, and I could make everybody laugh at themselves.

"Man, you must've grown up with a lot of black people," I constantly heard, "because you act black."

"Brother, I don't *act* anything; my father is black."

Immediately, demeanors changed: "Okay, now I get you! What's up, buddy?"

As far as basketball was concerned, I was a pretty decent player, so I quickly built some street cred with the other players. The counselors gave me a lot of praise, which was great for my self-esteem. The coaches, meanwhile, enforced the importance of showing up on time, not fooling around, and keeping our uniforms and practice gear neat and clean. The schedule was the same every day, with drills, scrimmage, and practice until late in the afternoon. As much as we were learning about the game, we were also learning about discipline. I was used to taking care of myself, but this was a different kind of responsibility. I had an alarm clock for the first time in my life. I had to get up on my own and get dressed. I had to shower and make it to scheduled mealtimes. I was held accountable.

Wes was very involved with the program, and he set the tone for the camp. He was a legend in the DC. area. At six foot seven and two hundred eighty pounds, he was a mountain of a man with a commanding presence. During our scrimmages, he sat on the sidelines and watched. I turned up my intensity every time I saw him watching; I wanted to impress him.

Sneakers squeaked against the hardwood as I chased after a rebound. We raced down the court in a mess of sweaty limbs and panting breath. Adrenaline pumped through my veins. My fingers itched to get ahold of the ball. I stayed with the guy I was guarding. I refused to let him shake me. He tried a fake pass, but I reached out and knocked the ball away with the tips of my fingers. I raced after it. My lungs burned as I brought it under control and thundered down the court in the opposite direction. The floorboards shook under the stampeding weight of the other nine players coming after me. My heart pounded as I drove in for the layup. I held my breath as I watched the ball go up. It bounced off the backboard, hit the center of the rim, and dropped through the net. Success!

Wes called a time-out. We trotted over to the bench, all of us trying to control our breathing so we could hear whatever he was going to say.

He smiled at me. "Way to go, kid. Keep it up."

I couldn't control my grin. "Thank you." I'd had tons of positive affirmation from my dad, but this was different. This was an NBA celebrity, and the attention felt extremely significant.

During lunch, the campers sat together watching Wes walk among us. Every so often, he stopped to talk to someone. I was laughing at one of my teammates when I felt a hand on my shoulder.

I looked up, way up, and saw Wes standing above me.

"How's everything going?"

Words failed me. He moved away through the crowd, stopping to talk to a few kids here and there. You could tell that he cared. He wasn't pretentious, and he was at the camp for the right reasons. Every time he spoke, he perpetuated an evangelical message about basketball, life, and the congruence of the two.

"Life is a team sport. You have to respect and look out for your teammates." We'd just finished our last scrimmage of the afternoon. Wes stood on the court, in front of the bleachers. All of us leaned forward, hanging on to every word. "You need to get along with a bunch of different people. We all come in with our different issues, our challenges, and our backgrounds, but all of us are stronger than one of us." He paused to look through the sea of players. "When you get knocked down, maybe you fall behind, but you've got to get up and keep fighting. Life will not stand still for you. You may be good today, but you have to keep improving and helping one another to be good tomorrow."

I wasn't reflective enough at the time to grasp all of the parallels he was drawing, but on the court I did feel as if we were all even. For the most part, race wasn't an issue. Our love of basketball evened the playing field. It didn't matter whether you were white, black, or otherwise; if you could play, you could contribute, and that was all that mattered.

There was a sense of independence at camp that freed me from the madness at home and allowed me to focus on something positive. We spent the nights in college dorms, either hanging out and playing games or watching movies. I listened for hours as the kids with beat-up tennis shoes talked about their skills in getting girls and skipping school and the guys with the brand new Nikes talked about watching pro games and going on vacations. Even though I felt a bond with my teammates and learned so much by seeing the world through their eyes, I kept my own thoughts and experiences to myself. My home life embarrassed me, and I always had my parents in my ear: "We don't talk about our business."

When I returned home after camp, everything was the same—but I had changed. I knew without a doubt that I wanted to play more sports. I had a little more confidence, and I felt more like an adult—or at least like an adolescent. I still tried to spend as little time inside the house as I could, leaving at eight a.m. and not returning until well after dinner. During the summer, I swam or played sports while Dad was at work.

Mom was home on the weekends, but she was either asleep or exhausted and she would leave me money for McDonald's instead of cooking. I wanted more stability at home, but I had developed a strong set of survival skills to deal with my world—a world, I finally recognized, I could escape through sports.

Despite my dad's positivity, both of my parents perpetuated the belief that our circumstances were just the hand we were dealt and that we had to live with it. Neither of them ever asked whether there was something we could do differently. Playing baseball and going to basketball camp gave me my first glimpse of what life could be with a different mindset.

CHAPTER 7

ALTERNATIVE EDUCATION

MOM WORKED THE GRAVEYARD SHIFT AT WASHINGTON HOSPITAL CENTER, so Dad and I spent many late weekend nights cruising in the car. We never had a particular destination; every trip was a new adventure, a new conversation, a new encounter. It was like paging through a coloring book and dragging my crayon outside the lines for the first time.

"The world is a dangerous place," Dad told me as he turned down 14th Street.

Hookers, drug dealers, and pimps in crazy outfits roamed the sidewalks. Gunshots punctuated the perpetual scream of police sirens. My heart pounded. Dad didn't seem nervous, though, so I played it cool.

"Take a look, Devin. This is what the world looks like sometimes." He pointed at a group of scantily dressed women standing on the curb near an intersection. "We all have choices. I've made some bad ones, and these women have made some of the same ones I did." He didn't say the world *school*, but I connected the dots between his life and theirs.

The Buick slowed as we rolled up to the corner. A couple of hookers ambled over, peering through the windshield at Dad.

He waved, rolling down his window. "How you ladies doing tonight?"

One of them smiled and bent down to talk to him. As soon as she caught sight of me, she backed away. "Nah, you're a freak. I don't do no kids."

"No, no, no, I just want to talk to you for a second."

"This ain't a circus. Keep moving."

"Come on, I just want to talk to you for a second."

"Why? I'm out here trying to make money and you want to *talk*?"

This was not a place where people with the highest moral values came on regular business, so the prostitutes were on their guard. None of them believed that someone would just want to talk to them.

Dad was patient with them. He kept his voice deliberate, made lots of eye contact, and smiled. Once he put her at ease, she returned to the driver's-side window and leaned her forearms on the open frame. I stared out the windshield, avoiding looking at my dad or the woman while they chatted. After a few minutes, I heard a rustle of cloth among the conversation and glanced over. My mouth fell open: her arm was all the way in the car, her hand on my dad's crotch. She kept massaging him as he asked her questions about her life. I covered my eyes with my hands, but I couldn't help peeking through my fingers to see what happened next. Dad never flinched. He didn't say anything; he rolled with it like a ballroom dancer on his first spin with a new partner—the body may have been different, but the dance was familiar.

During these trips, questions flew through my mind. *How does an attractive girl end up a streetwalker? What is it like sleeping with strange men? Do your parents know you're out here? Will you ever quit?* I was too scared to ask. However, by the third or fourth time, I looked forward to going back.

One young woman stands out in my memories of these trips. She looked like Farrah Fawcett, whose picture hung on my bedroom wall; she didn't match the abrasive, unkempt image of a hooker I had in my head. She was sweet and soft-spoken—the girl next door. While Dad talked to one of the other prostitutes, Farrah's look-alike walked over to my side of the car.

"What are you doing out here?" she asked.

I replied with a line I'd learned from my dad. "How are you doing tonight?"

She laughed. "You don't want to be out here with us folks." A sad smile curled the corners of her lips.

I ignored the soft conversation going on at the other side of the car. This girl seemed so nice and polite. There was a cognitive dissonance in seeing someone so young and beautiful in this environment; it didn't make sense to me. I gathered up the courage to ask the question that had been on my mind since my first encounter with the hookers. "Why are you out here?"

She sighed. "It's a long story. This isn't the life, kid. You have to listen to your dad and stay in school."

When I think about the life lessons I picked up in my adventures with my father, I always recall that conversation: "Look at me and look what I have done," she was saying. "I was you once, and you have a choice." Her message was the same one I heard from my parents, pushing me not to be like them, to aspire to more.

On our rides home, Dad always picked up where he'd left off with the conversation before we hit 14th Street.

"See, Devin, with an education, you can make your own decisions and your own choices. You're not stuck like your pops is."

I never asked why he took me, and we never talked

about the trips once we got home. I just assumed they were part of the journey, part of my ghetto-fabulous schooling. He helped me visualize the consequences of choices he didn't want me to make. I never mentioned these outings to anyone. I was embarrassed, but I was also guarded. I always had my parents' warning about not trusting anyone in the back of my mind. To this day, I don't know if my mom knew about these trips.

My father exposed me to as much as he could within his limited resources. We went to cultural fairs all over DC. It didn't matter whether it was a special history exhibit at the Smithsonian or a Native American fair at the mall; Dad took me to all of them. He'd dropped out of high school halfway through his freshman year, but he was always reading. Nonfiction books littered the apartment—everything from biographies and histories to books about spirituality and the Black Panthers. He read everything he could get his hands on in his quest to leave his past behind. I paged through some of them to see what he got out of them, but the small print was strung together in so many long sentences that I couldn't make sense of them.

On a Sunday morning, Mom had just gotten home from work and shut herself in the bedroom. Dad had a book in hand as he paced back and forth in front of the TV.

"They thought I would never amount to shit," he said to himself. "I was just the little red nigger who was going to be an alcoholic like his mom."

I ignored him and tried to focus on my show. Dad used the word *nigger* all the time, but I never felt comfortable with the word. I had decided that fifty percent wasn't black enough to use it.

Dad snapped the book shut and continued pacing. "We'll show them."

Over the last few months, his energy level had been low. His familiar high-pitched laughs were now few and far between. I guessed I understood: at work, he dealt with racism on a daily basis. At home, he and Mom had formed a symbiotic relationship that only worked around me, the lynchpin. Right now, as restless as he was, he seemed more present, more like his old self. I didn't understand the change, but I would roll with it.

He stopped pacing and looked at me. "Get up. We're going to church."

"What?" I didn't know what to think. We had never gone to church as far as I could remember, except once or twice at his family reunions in South Carolina. "Is Mom going?"

"No. Just you and me."

"Why?"

"Don't ask me why. Just put on your sport coat and your nice pants and let's go."

"I have to dress up? Oh, man." I dragged my feet all the way to my room.

"I've been in and out of Catholic churches all my life, Devin," he said on our way over. "It's time for you to go, and me to get back." He'd stopped going to church regularly when a priest in Knoxville solicited him for sex. Dad wasn't shy about telling me this sort of thing.

My first impression on walking through the doors of St. Patrick's was that the church was very white. Sterile white walls stretched high overhead. White people filled the pews; I felt the eyes of rows and rows of motionless white mannequins turn to us. Dad was the only color in the room.

I followed Dad to a pew at the back and slid into the very end. The back of the pew in front of us provided just enough cover for me to duck behind. Whispers flew through the congregation, creating a mild buzz in the air. I snuck peeks at the people sitting around us. Left, right, forward, back—I tried to keep my eyes on all of them. According to my parents, I couldn't trust anyone, and already I had a habit of taking note of my surroundings at all times. By this time I had a little experience with white people, but at school and at basketball camp, I was comfortable with the environment and there were always a lot of black kids. Here, I didn't know the people or the surroundings; I didn't have a comfort zone. I was behind enemy lines again.

What is she thinking? I wondered as a woman in front of us turned and looked over her shoulder. *Black man, white kid? What's that all about?* Someone two rows up looked back. *Is that guy staring?* I tried to catch his eye, but he looked away. Pretending not to notice, I grabbed the songbook in front of me. I could pick out only a few familiar words on each page. I glanced back at the man, who had turned around again. Again, he averted his eyes.

Everyone stood up as music swelled from the piano. The priest and a couple of boys in robes walked up the aisle.

"Get up," Dad said in a loud whisper.

I didn't want to stand, but I didn't want to draw any more attention either, though Dad didn't seem to notice the mannequins looking at us. I hauled myself to my feet, and the priest started talking. The whole congregation responded. I couldn't even tell what they said. Then everyone sat. They all seemed to know what to do, but the formality felt alien to me. When the music started again, everybody shifted to their feet. Dad swayed with the beat. He shook his head back and forth.

"Amen, brother," he said to the man next to him. "Amen!"

I didn't know what to make of this. No one else talked. No one else swayed. No one else moved at all. I put my head down. All I wanted to do was punch the spiritual time clock, maybe give a high five to the Lord, and sneak out, but here was Dad, having some kind of transcendent experience. Was this real? I didn't feel anything. None of the white people around us looked as if they felt anything. Maybe this was what my dad thought church should be, but I couldn't see a method to his madness.

True to form, we didn't talk about it on the ride home. Dad turned to me as he slid behind the wheel. "So, do you think the Redskins are going to win today?"

"Maybe." I rolled the window down and stuck my face into the wind. I couldn't wait to take off the sport coat. Church didn't make sense. How could all those people act one way in church, and then turn around and be the biggest bigots in the outside world? My mom's father had gone to church, I knew. Some of the folks that Dad worked with did, too, he said, but their behavior toward him wasn't exactly being good to your fellow man. Even Dad I couldn't figure out; he was sitting right there next to me singing about virtue and faithfulness, but at home he smoked pot and took me to visit prostitutes.

When we got home, Mom was still asleep in her room. I changed my clothes and went out to play.

Dad worked a lot of Sundays for double time, so church never became a regular thing. We only went to St. Patrick's that one time before Dad moved us to a Methodist parish.

The Methodist church was not as sterile as the Catholic one. Inside, the walls were a nondescript beige, and I was relieved to see more color in the congregation. There was also less formality, so Dad didn't stick out as much during the service. Still, without the context for why it was important to go to church, I went into an hour-long catatonic daydream state. Dad must not have found what he was looking for here, either, because we never went back. It was like going to a restaurant and sampling one item on the menu, then moving on to the next place.

Our next experiment was a Southern Baptist church. This time, I was the only white face in an entirely black congregation. The people here dressed to impress. The Catholics had worn nice clothes, too, but they didn't hold a candle to the loud colors of the hats, dresses, and suits at the Baptist church.

Service was animated, dramatic, with lots of singing, dancing, and yelling. People moved in and out of the pews while the preacher shouted at us. All around me, arms were raised to the sky. The smell of sweat permeated the air. Ladies fanned themselves with bulletins.

"Praise Jesus!" someone behind me shouted.

"God bless you, son," a stranger said as she hugged me.

I looked at Dad to see what I should do, but he was dancing and smiling, totally present, as though he had been doing this all his life. *What does he feel that I don't feel?* This was a circus, and I watched the acts in bewilderment. Everyone kept trying to pull me into the performance, but I wanted to be in the audience. The dichotomy between the Catholic and Baptist experiences was profound. I was just as much an outsider in each.

Soon after this service, I was at the grocery store where Dad was ready to get off work. On the way out, we ran into a guy named Nat Randolph. Short and weasely with a scraggly beard, Nat was an ardent follower of Louis Farrakhan and the Nation of Islam.

"As-salamu alaykum, my brother," Nat said to Dad. "Did you see the news? The white man—"

I tuned him out. Every time I met him, all he did was complain about what the black man couldn't do because the white man kept him down. With all the racism Dad faced at work, he was naturally drawn to the message—but that was half my DNA Nat was talking about! He had to see that I wasn't completely black, but my dad would have lit him up if he said directly anything against me.

Nat kept talking. "Louis Farrakhan is going to be in town next week. You should come check it out. It's all about black empowerment." He handed Dad a copy of

Malcolm X's book, then looked at me. "Bring the kid. It'll be good for him."

Dad nodded attentively. He never egged Nat on, but he soaked up all the information like a sponge. "Yeah. Yeah, I'll do that."

The next week, we went to see Louis Farrakhan speak. We walked into the conference hall, and I stopped in my tracks. There were at least five hundred people there, every one of them black. *Everyone*, except me—I was a little marshmallow in a bowl of Hershey's Kisses. It seemed no matter where we went, I was on the outside looking in. I was beginning to doubt that I fit in anywhere.

We navigated the crowd and found a place to stand near the back. I tried to turn invisible while observing the people around me. Everyone was dressed to the nines; onstage, the men wore bow ties and red hats with tassels.

"In the name of Allah, the beneficent, the merciful," a voice boomed.

All around, people fell silent, transfixed. I didn't know who Allah was, or if he was the same god to which the Catholics and the Methodists prayed. Religion seemed like Baskin-Robbins—so many different flavors, it was impossible that only one could be right. The peace in the conference hall didn't last long.

"You have not come here for Louis Farrakhan," he said. "You have gathered here at the call of Almighty God, for only He could generate this outpouring."

The man's energy infused the crowd. Several men in the audience shouted back. "Yeah, brother! That's right!"

The audience grew louder and more frenzied as Farrakhan kept talking.

"The black man doesn't stand a chance!"

"The white man is to blame!"

I was scared, but I buried that fear deep inside. These messages were so incongruent with my own reality. I snuck a look at Dad, wondering whether he was thinking about Mom while everyone around us shouted about the evil of white people. Dad stood there, rapt attention radiating from his face. The meeting didn't end until late in the night.

On the way out to the car, a million questions flew through my head. Why do we even need a priest or a preacher? Why do I need a conduit to connect to an all-powerful being? Did Louis Farrakhan somehow have a deeper connection to God than the rest of us?

As we drove away, I finally asked, "Why do they talk about white people so much? Why are they so angry?" I didn't ask the other questions that weighed heavily on my mind. "Do I have to go back?"

"This is important stuff for you to hear, Devin. You got to know where you come from," Dad said, not directly answering my question.

Dad was fired up with the Black Power movement. He went to meetings regularly, very interested in getting more involved with Islam. After a few months, however, his excitement fizzled.

"This is bullshit," he said, throwing a handful of papers onto the already cluttered kitchen table. "These niggers aren't no different than anybody else. They're just talking a bunch of nonsense. How many times can you hear the white man does this, and the white man does that?"

He stomped off toward the bathroom.

"They're going to keep complaining about the white man and never get to black empowerment." The bathroom door slammed shut behind him.

I shuffled through the papers he dropped on the table. He met all kinds of people at the grocery store, and he never turned down an invitation when they asked him to try their church or offered information about their faith. The papers were more religious pamphlets. At least I assumed they were all religious—they were full of long words I didn't recognize. One phrase in particular was repeated in several of the pamphlets. Maybe if I could understand that, I could guess at what the rest of the papers said. That was what I did at school—build context from a couple of words or phrases.

The toilet flushed, and Dad stormed back into the kitchen as I picked up a bright yellow pamphlet. A peace sign was stamped on the front. "What does this mean?" I asked, pointing to the two words I couldn't read.

"Spiritual enlightenment," Dad said. "We're going to go find out." He snatched up the pamphlet and his keys. Just like that, he was done with Islam. So far, none of the religions he'd tried had led him to the secret sauce for fulfillment. He must have hoped this one would be the game-changer.

I followed him down to the car, a little apprehensive about this next adventure. He might have been looking for salvation, but he also wanted me to feel comfortable being uncomfortable; that was always one of his priorities. That made me nervous.

The ride was a short, silent one. We parked at the curb outside a small home on the other end of Silver Spring. I followed Dad up the walk. My heart pounded as hard against my ribs as his fist did against the door.

A middle-aged white man with a messy mane of hair cracked open the door. "Can I help you?"

Dad held up the pamphlet. "We met at the A&P the other day. We're here for the Buddhist worship service."

"Right, of course." The man grinned. A low humming noise drifted out from somewhere inside as he swung the door open wide. "Come in, come in."

The humming grew louder and more distinct as he ushered us into a large living room. All of the furniture had been moved out of the room. The source of the humming turned out to be a dozen people sitting cross-legged in a horseshoe-shaped ring on the brown shag carpet, chanting the same phrase over and over.

"Nam myoho renge kyo, nam myoho renge kyo."

The lights were off, but a few candles set up in the middle threw flickering light. This was unlike any of the other religions we had tried before. Here I saw Asians, Hispanics, whites, blacks, short, tall, fat, thin, old, young, but I was the only kid. The only common thread was a look of dishevelment and unkempt hair. The sweet stench of incense tickled my nostrils and fogged the air of the dark room. Two of the chanters moved over, and Dad and I sat down between them.

I didn't know what to do. At least in church, I knew I was supposed to look forward and pay attention. Here, everyone had their eyes closed, but I couldn't help staring directly at the crazy hippies. The man who had answered the door folded his legs beneath him and dropped back into his spot at the top of the horseshoe.

"Welcome to our circle," he said with another grin. "*Nam myoho renge kyo* is the expression of the laws of life which all Buddhist teachings in one way or another seek to clarify." He started chanting with the rest of them.

Dad became Captain Buddha and joined right in, his voice louder than anybody else's even though he didn't know any more than I did what all of this meant. The woman to my left started swaying side to side, bumping into my shoulder as she moaned provocatively. I scooted as far to my right as I could without leaning against Dad. I kept my mouth shut and waited for the night to be over so I could retreat to the safety of the car. Out of all the religions we'd tried, this one made the least sense to me.

On the way home I asked a rare question. "Pops, what's up with that stuff in there?" I leaned my forehead against the window. "I mean, sitting on the floor, Indian style, chanting—why do they do that?"

Dad shrugged and laughed. "Yeah, that was crazy, wasn't it?"

We never went back.

For a year, my father went through religions like he went through underwear, and he brought me along for the ride. We ate from every dish at the religious buffet: Presbyterianism, Buddhism, Hinduism and its Hare Krishnas, and every other derivative imaginable. I learned to see the world from many different perspectives and found more questions than answers. I couldn't comprehend how all of these religions could coexist; there couldn't be that many gods.

I got to the point where I expected all our car rides to end up at a church of some sort. When Mom came home from work Sunday mornings, it was time to go.

Mom came through the front door, a bag of fast food crumpled in one hand. She threw the food and her purse on the table and lit a cigarette. A sigh escaped her lips. Dad barely acknowledged her. He gave her a wide berth on his way to grab his keys.

"Do I have to dress up today?" I asked, thinking I knew what came next.

"No. We're not going to church today."

Mom narrowed her eyes as she inhaled. "Where are you going this time?"

The tension in the room ratcheted up a notch. It felt as if we were falling headfirst into an old argument that they never resolved.

"We're going over to Aunt Fanny's."

I held my breath. Aunt Fanny's house was in a neighborhood even the hookers on 14th wouldn't frequent. That place didn't just make me uncomfortable; it scared me. The animosity between my parents grew into something palpable as they stared each other down. I didn't want to stick around and find out how this would end, but I hated going to Aunt Fanny's. Dad wanted me to make good choices, but everything was out of my control. The ominous silence continued for seconds that felt like hours.

Finally, Dad broke the stillness. "Devin, let's go."

CHAPTER 8

DIAGNOSIS: DYSLEXIA

BESIDES THEIR NAMES, I DIDN'T KNOW MUCH ABOUT AUNT FANNY AND HER KIDS. From watching TV, I thought family should make you want to be open and engage, to love and connect with other people, but when Dad whispered in my ear all of the bad things Fanny's family was tied up in, I couldn't make them fit the picture I had in my head. I never connected with any of them even though we went to her place at least once or twice a month, bringing groceries or running errands for her.

The trip took at least forty-five minutes one way. I slouched in the backseat, my arms folded over my chest as I watched the neighborhoods worsen the closer we got.

"I hate going to Fanny's."

Dad glanced at me in the rearview mirror. "She's a good old girl. She needs my help."

"But why do you keep dragging me along?"

"We won't stay long." He always said that.

"There's nothing to do there." I kept up my litany without ever telling him the real reason I didn't want to go. Her house represented the seedy underbelly of DC. This was beyond the hookers on 14th Street—there, everything was out in the open, no pretense. At Fanny's, there was too much of a disconnect between what I felt family should be and the reality that presented itself. I had enough chaos in my life without absorbing any of theirs.

Dad turned to me as we pulled up in front of the house. "Son, I don't want you turning out like Fanny's boys, you hear me?" The "boys," his cousins, were approximately his age, the oldest only a few years his senior and the youngest no more than eight years his junior.

"Then why do we come over here?"

He kept talking as if I hadn't said anything. "They aren't going to amount to anything in life, Devin."

My skin crawled when he stopped the car. Fanny's house of horrors was at the center of a lot of questionable activity. It had been a refuge for my mom when she ran away, but it was only slightly more comforting than living on the street. If I had known what a crack house was at the time, that's how I would've described it. Bullet holes riddled the walls; no one ever bothered to patch them. I never knew exactly who lived in the house and who was just passing through.

We walked up the front steps. Dad knocked on the door and walked inside. Fanny's loud voice carried down the hallway from a room in the back of the house. On the way to the back room, we passed several closed bedroom doors. The doors only muffled the music and shouting, mashing all the noise into a pulsing cacophony that seemed to be the lifeblood of the house.

Aunt Fanny sat in a recliner, talking business with a handful of people I recognized but didn't know. Rumor had it that her husband had been a gambler until the day he got himself tossed off the roof of an office building in DC. for cheating in a card game. Fanny was a large, heavyset black woman, an authoritarian matriarch who spun every situation to her advantage. The consummate mafioso, she granted favors and gave advice in exchange for future assistance. At any given time, she held the strings of dozens of puppets, one of which was my father.

The conversation fell silent when we entered the room. I sensed we had walked into the middle of some sort of transaction. Once again, mine was the only white face in the room.

"You should go out back and play, Devin," Fanny told me.

I plastered a fake smile on my face and shook my head. I thought of the bullet holes in the exterior walls. Were the people who put them there coming back?

"He's so shy," one of the men said. He reminded me of Fanny's son Jackie; he fidgeted constantly and wore tons of flashy jewelry—a celebrity-gangster wannabe. "Clarkie, you have to get that boy out more. He doesn't talk enough."

All eyes in the room turned to me.

Dad brushed the comment aside. "Don't worry about him. He'll be fine."

"There are some neighborhood kids down the block," Fanny tried again. "Just go see if anyone is outside."

"No, I'm good. I want to hang out here." *Liar.* I didn't want to leave Dad's side.

Dad didn't seem to feel the weight of the stares directed at us. "You said you needed me to run an errand?"

"Mayo has work-release," Fanny replied. Mayo was Jackie's older brother. "I need you to go pick him up and drive him."

Dad nodded. "Sure, no problem."

Just like that, Fanny flicked her wrist and sent her puppets into a dance; we were on our way to prison.

Since his childhood, Dad's relationship with his own mother had been tumultuous at best. By the time he was a teenager, he knew she had a reputation for being a floozy. She disappeared often after going on drinking binges, but he still felt love from her and valued her a great deal, and that was something he missed. Since leaving home, he'd yearned for a mother figure, and he felt an obligation to Fanny for giving my mom a place to stay when she first moved to DC. He also wanted validation for having made something of his life.

Before Dad had left home, he'd spent a few summers harvesting tobacco with his mom at one of the local farms in North Carolina. They lived in shacks on the edge of the property with sixty other workers. All day long they picked tobacco, and at night they gathered around a makeshift stove in the barn and ate biscuits and fatback. Their beds were grain sacks stuffed with hay. Dad had a hard time falling asleep, because he was afraid a snake or giant bug would pounce on him as soon as he closed his eyes. After spending a summer with my redneck grandfather, I knew well that fear of drifting off.

When Dad's mom disappeared on a drinking binge, he lived with the family that told him, "A little red nigger won't amount to anything." Like me, Dad spent his childhood feeling isolated, as if he never fit in. He went through life believing he had something to prove to everyone, Fanny included. He sought approval that his life had turned out okay; he had a job, a nice car, and a family, and Fanny's boys didn't.

Her son Jackie had tried to rob a Japanese steakhouse, and on his way out he shot the proprietor, who shot back with a small-caliber handgun. Jackie made it to the hospital five bullet holes richer, and the store owner died. Jackie didn't want the doctors to remove the bullets because he didn't want them matched to the dead man's gun.

"Jackie's a heroin addict and a criminal," Dad said when we were back in the car. "He always used to make fun of me for having a job and living at home like a white man while he was out hustling. Mayo isn't any better."

"Then why are we helping him?"

"He's been dealing and hustling and breaking the law for a long time. His luck just ran out. He's still family."

Lorton Reformatory was a giant, formidable structure of concrete and barbed wire that loomed over us as we drove by. White men in uniforms stood along the walls and in the towers, big guns clenched in their hands. We arrived at the gate where Dad had to check in with the guards. The barrel-chested gate guard leaned toward Dad's window.

"Photo ID, sir."

"Good morning, officer." Dad handed over his driver's license, all smiles.

The guard didn't smile back. "State your business." I could see myself in his mirrored sunglasses when he peered into the back of the car. What was he thinking?

"We're here to drive a few of the inmates to work-release in the city."

The man handed the license back and waved us through. More uniforms waited to escort us from the car to the doors and into a holding room. None of the guards smiled at me. They all seemed tense, just waiting from somebody to act so they could react. As we waited, Dad assumed an air of cocky bravado—the same attitude that had gotten him through his stint behind bars helped him keep the upper hand with the guys we were here to pick up. More guards ushered Mayo and three other large black men in street clothes into the holding area and signed them over to Dad. Everyone was quiet until we got outside. Only then did the prisoners loosen up a little and start joking with one another.

Dad became the alpha dog right away. The tone and inflection of his voice took on a tough, stern edge that I had never heard from him before.

"Sit your asses down and be quiet," he commanded.

Mayo climbed into the front seat, and I had to share the back with the other three convicts. I pressed myself against the door as hard as I could, but my arm and leg still touched the guy next to me. Even though they were all bigger than Dad, they accepted his lead.

"Keep your head down and no fooling around," Dad said. "I don't want to be fooling in front of the cops."

Once we rolled past the prison gates, the guys were engaging and likeable. I would even call them nice. If I hadn't just seen them ushered out of prison, I never would have known they were criminals. The trip into DC was just like sitting around the stoop at home.

"So what's going on out here?" one of the cons asked.

"Yeah, how are the Redskins this year?" another chimed in.

It was normal small talk you might have with anyone on the street, except it was prisoners in the car with us. Dad didn't seem uncomfortable; he had no problems assimilating into seedy culture. The people he'd hung out with as a younger man were of a very low rung on the social and economic ladders. Dad was one of them, and he represented someone who had arrived, or escaped, even though everyone said he would be a drunken loser like his mom. He was also the constant victim of racism and bullying, and he was always willing to help anyone who needed him; it was his way of giving back to the community. I supposed a combination of desires—for validation and to help—were why we were doing this.

Eventually, one of the guys said, "Man, what would happen if you came to pick us up later and we're not there?"

My heart stopped for a beat, then started pumping double time. There were four of them and only two of us. Would they try to take over the car? Were they joking?

Dad's demeanor instantly changed. "If you're stupid enough to try to escape now, you are a damn fool. I'm going to be there, and your asses better be there, too, because I'm not covering for you." He didn't miss a beat, just assumed control of the situation and moved on.

After we dropped them off, we drove to the A&P and Dad worked until it was time to pick them up and take them back to Lorton.

Fanny called at least once every other week looking for favors like that. My dad's habit of jumping at Fanny's every whim irritated my mother. It was the topic of many heated arguments.

"Why the hell do you keep running over there every time she calls?" Mom stood before the front door, arms crossed and eyes blazing. "She's just using your dumb ass."

Dad grabbed his keys and made for the door. "You don't know what the hell you're talking about. She's my aunt. She's been good to me."

"She's been good to you? She has your ass running all over DC doing favors for her!"

He shoved Mom out of the way and didn't say another word. The door slammed after him, adding the final punctuation to the exchange.

Feeling needed was part of the relationship that Dad hadn't experienced with his mother, so no matter how hard my mom tried to convince him that Fanny was just using him, he stubbornly insisted that she needed his help. One day, though, Fanny pulled the wrong string.

"You must think I'm stupid!" he shouted into the phone. "I'm not going to risk everything I got to slip drugs into prison for Jackie." The request had shone a light on what my mother had been saying all along: this wasn't love; it was manipulation.

Outside of Fanny's house, I trusted Dad's judgment. It was Mom I didn't trust completely; I had doubts that she would do the right thing for the family, because she could be so focused on herself and disconnected from the rest of us. It wasn't until I started struggling in school that I realized how far she would go to help me succeed.

Dad had books around the apartment, but he told me everything he wanted me to know. Neither he nor Mom read to me, so reading wasn't a habit I had picked up. Spelling was okay because I could just memorize words. Writing a simple paragraph, however, was torture.

I skipped over or duplicated words, and my punctuation was appalling. I could study five minutes before a test and score perfectly, then get the same questions wrong on subsequent written assignments. I didn't understand the material, but I could memorize like crazy so I coped without comprehending. At the age of eight, I became a world-class professional fake reader. If the material was read out loud, I memorized how it sounded and then connected the dots to what it looked like on paper. I worked on excuses for my bad grades in between marking periods and learned to memorize words quickly in the interim. Still, despite my parents' belief in my high potential, I was struggling. Some unknown force prevented me from reading and writing at the same pace as the other kids, and it crushed the self-esteem that sports had built. I knew something was wrong. Instead of making myself vulnerable and asking for help, I disassociated myself and went into that familiar there-but-not-there catatonic state where I became an observer instead of a participant.

I dreaded reading hour. A special aide walked into the room at ten o'clock and two o'clock on the dot every day. She walked up and down the rows of desks, stopping to whisper in a few students' ears. The class was made up of at least two dozen other kids, and five of us were sequestered with that aide every day. My four fellow detainees wilted visibly when she reached their places. They resigned themselves to a slow death march to the back of the room, where an accordion wall slid back to reveal a small side area. I felt every snicker of my classmates—the aide wasn't fooling anyone with her whispering. We all felt the ignominy; everyone could read the scarlet letters tattooed across the slow learners' foreheads.

"Devin," the aide whispered in my ear. "Devin, you too."

I took a deep breath and ran to the back of the room as fast as I could. Maybe no one would notice.

On the other side of the wall, the five of us sat in an uncomfortable circle with the aide. Even when she talked, we could hear the other students in class on the other side of the flimsy divider.

"All right, class, settle down." The teacher's voice drifted through the wall, slightly muffled. "Turn your books to page forty-three."

I looked down at the reading book. We were on page thirteen. My mind wandered as the aide pointed to one of the truly bad readers.

His face turned red, and his forehead furrowed. "The—the—the—the b-b-b-boy," he began. He stuttered at least three times on every word.

I looked around the group of misfits. Some of them couldn't remember how to pronounce simple words two minutes after being shown, or how to differentiate nouns from verbs, even though we'd been drilling for weeks. *These kids belong here*, I thought. I was struggling a little bit, but I didn't fit in with this group. The whole experience tasted like a peanut butter sandwich that just didn't have enough peanut butter on it, but I had to choke it down or starve.

I hated going to school, but I had developed the ability to hide my emotions to avoid being perceived as weak. If anyone tried to make fun of me, I tore them up with words, the way I had learned from Mom's deadly verbal assaults. She knew how to dig into someone's insecurities to break them down emotionally. I did the same thing to other students and to the teacher. Being likeable and athletic also worked to my advantage; I was always making people laugh and looking for ways to fit in. To others, it probably appeared that I had everything going for me, but in truth, I was dying a slow death. I was on the outside looking in, a con artist and a fraud, but I had everyone fooled—including my parents. They didn't know for months that I had been put in the slow class. It wasn't until I received a particular report card that Mom's radar started blinking.

"What's with this report card, Devin?" Mom pinned me with a piercing gaze she usually reserved for her fights with Dad. We sat at the kitchen table, the offending paper sitting between us.

I shrugged. "The grades aren't that bad."

"I'm not worried about the grades. Why does it say you're acting up in class?"

"It's not my fault. I can't see the board." I couldn't look her in the eyes.

"You've had your eyes checked half a dozen times. That's not the problem."

"It's boring."

"That's not an excuse."

"The teacher doesn't get me."

Mom drummed her fingers against the table. "Don't give me that. What's really wrong?"

"I don't know!"

She sighed. Her voice softened. "Devin, you know

what's expected of you in school, right?"

"Yeah."

"Then why are you clowning around in class?"

I threw my hands in the air. "Everything is harder than it should be, and I have no idea why." I gathered enough courage to look her in the face as I admitted my shameful secret. "They put me in a special class with the slow kids."

Light frown lines creased her forehead. For once, she looked interested.

After that conversation, she started checking over my assignments; she had never really helped me with my homework before, but now she was like a private detective inspecting my work for clues. It didn't take long for her to spot my habit of repeating words.

"Here, Devin," she said, handing one of my written papers to me. "Read this and tell me if there's anything wrong with this paragraph."

I scanned my own handwriting. "No. It looks fine."

She took the paper from me and pointed to a spot where I had written *"The boy crossed crossed the street."*

The realization struck me like a physical blow. It felt as if the world had stopped rotating for a moment. "Mom, I didn't see that word before." How had I missed this? Was I really dumb?

"I know, honey. It's okay." She smiled at me. A smile— a real smile just for me! "We're going to figure out what this is."

Her reassurance made me feel better, but I still felt the scar of that *aha* moment. Now that she pointed it out, I saw that I had repeated words in multiple assignments. How could I not have seen this before? Why did I do it?

A work friend of Mom's had a contact at the University of Maryland who knew something about testing for learning disabilities. Mom made a couple of phone calls and scheduled an appointment to bring me in on a Saturday morning. I badly wanted Mom's attention, so I didn't object to having to spend half a day doing tests.

We sat in the car in silence on the way to the university. Snippets of morning radio show reruns blared over the sound of traffic. I was nervous. Mom hadn't said anything all morning. Her face was serious.

"What are we going to do there?" I asked for the millionth time since she'd told me I had an appointment.

She sighed. "Just be quiet and go with it. We're going to be fine."

I looked out the window and watched the cars go by, wondering what lay ahead. I wanted more information, but Mom didn't know much more than I did.

We rolled into a large parking lot outside the university. Mom turned off the radio. She looked at me.

"We're going to find out what might be precluding you from being the best you can be, okay? We all learn differently. It's okay to be different."

I nodded.

"It will be fine. This is a good thing."

I didn't know whether she was reassuring me or herself. In some ways I didn't want to be diagnosed with a problem, because I had no context for what that would mean, yet at the same time I wanted a hall pass to show that it wasn't me, that I wasn't stupid, that there was something else going on.

We got out of the car. On the way to the front door, Mom grabbed my hand. She hadn't done that since she dropped me off at nursery school for the first time. My mind raced with questions. Why was she trying to comfort me? Did I need comforting for what was about to happen? What if they came back with a diagnosis that was permanent? I walked into the office with a basketball-sized lump of worry sitting in my gut. Mom checked me in and we sat in the lobby to wait, both of us retreating into our own heads.

"Devin Hughes," an assistant called.

I slowly got to my feet and followed the woman. She was white. Everyone at the university seemed to be white. Mom stayed in the lobby. The assistant led me to a small classroom with green office carpet and white walls. A white woman sat at a metal desk and smiled at me when I walked in.

"Hi, Devin," she said. "I'm so glad you came. This is a great step."

I asked her the same question I'd been asking Mom all week. "What are we going to do? Am I going to be okay?"

"Absolutely." She pointed to a desk across from hers. "Have a seat."

I sat. My nerves fired into overdrive. "Am I going to be okay?" I couldn't help asking again.

The woman came over to my desk. "I've heard all about you from your mom. It sounds like you have a lot of things to offer, and you're a very special young man."

Mom had said that? I could hardly believe my ears.

"God gives us all different talents and sometimes we have to work with each other to help pull those gifts out. We're going to figure out how to make you the best that you can be. Are you up for the challenge?"

Her words validated what my mom had said in the car. Maybe it *was* okay to be different. "I'm in," I said. "Let's do this."

The tests weren't intimidating. For one of them, I had to pick out the right words to finish sentences; for another, I had to read a few paragraphs out loud. They seemed more like games than tests.

"Just fly through it naturally," the woman said as she handed me a sheet of paper. "Don't spend too much time on it; just go instinctively."

After the tests were finished, I walked back out to the lobby with much more excitement than I'd walked in with. Mom told me to wait while she talked to the woman who had administered the tests. I tried to listen, but I couldn't hear what they were saying.

"How did it go?" Mom asked on the way out to the car.

"It went great! Now what are we going to do?"

"We're done now. We're going home, and in a few weeks we'll come back and get the results."

That was that. We didn't talk about it until the diagnosis came back ten days later. We had to go back to the university to talk to the staff. This time Mom seemed more nervous than I was.

We sat in the white woman's office, the two of us on one side, her on the other. She smiled at us.

"Devin has a mild disability called dyslexia."

It was a relief to hear there was a name for my problem, but I was almost indifferent to the news—okay, I'm dyslexic, great. Now what? Most of the conversation was over my head, so I let Mom handle it.

"What does that mean?" she asked.

"Dyslexia can cause struggles with reading and writing—"

"Where does it come from? Is it curable? What does this mean long term?" Mom fired off a barrage of questions, barely giving the woman enough time to answer one before asking another. Mom was crusading on my behalf, and I felt closer to her than I ever had.

"What tools or resources can you recommend for us?" Mom was on a mission. It was awesome to see her in action, driving toward a goal. She was stepping up in a much more polished way than my pistol-carrying father, and even though she was uneducated, you could tell how bright she was from how she spoke. From her, I learned how to frame a conversation and to be deliberate with my words and intentions. Mom's body language and eye contact kept her present in the moment; she was nothing like the exhausted, glassy-eyed woman she usually was at home, and I was proud of the way she handled herself. This was a side of her that I didn't get to see often.

The woman gave us a list of names of people who could work with me. On the way out of her office, both Mom and I were in high spirits. We had a plan.

CHAPTER 9

SOCIAL ARCHEOLOGY

AFTER A MONTH OF MAKING INQUIRIES, Mom found a private school with a teacher who tutored kids as a side job. Linda agreed to tutor me after school and on weekends. The first time we visited the school, Mom came with me. The room where we met the tutor was huge. Toys cluttered the shelves. There were basketball hoops hung high on one of the walls. This was completely different than the classrooms I associated with learning. I was happy simply to have found an answer for why I was struggling, but *this*—if the toys and basketball hoops were any indication—was going to be fantastic.

My tutor was a short, heavyset white woman. Her butt was enormous, as were her yellow teeth, and her hair was cut extremely short. She was an odd-looking woman, but she immediately made me feel warm and comfortable; the way she framed the issue of my dyslexia was genius.

"It's not a question of your ability, Devin." Her breath smelled like old cigarettes and old coffee, kind of like Mom's.

"But I'm in the dumb group."

"We're all born with a different set of gifts." She used the word *gift* often. With her, dyslexia was never presented as a disability. "You're not dumb—you just see the world through a unique set of lenses."

In hindsight, my lenses weren't just those of dyslexia but also those of a boy from a lower class, biracial family. My lenses were those of a boy who was always around thugs and seedy people, disconnected from family. My lenses were those of a boy who felt different from everyone around him, isolated from everyone due to circumstances outside of his control. Dyslexia was just the latest set I was learning to see through.

One of the first things Linda did was present me with a list of famous dyslexics, like Thomas Edison and Walt Disney—a shrewd move on her part. She wanted me to visualize a light at the end of the scholastic tunnel, and it worked. I had something in common with people I admired. Now I was different in a good way, eclectic. It was still isolating to feel as if no one else I *knew* saw the world the way I did, but I started to feel better about my situation.

I saw Linda twice a week, and she gave me homework between sessions. In the beginning of our relationship, I skipped the assignments as often as I did them. I tested her boundaries and my ability to sniff out weaknesses. No matter what I tried, she didn't let me off the hook.

"Look, Devin," she said the second time I handed her an incomplete assignment. "The expectation is that when I ask you to do something, you are going to have it done by our next session."

I fell right back into my habit of making excuses. "I was busy."

"Busy doing what?"

I shrugged. I wasn't prepared for follow-up questioning.

"What is more important than helping yourself succeed?" She paused for a moment, waiting for me to respond. "Do you *want* to succeed? If you don't, tell me right now. I'll call your mom and we can stop doing this. She'll thank me for saving her a bunch of money."

Linda's gaze was direct and honest, the way my dad's was when he coached our baseball team. Like him, she wasn't out to embarrass me or make me feel bad about myself; she wanted to help me, to challenge me to perform at my best. I responded to that kind of talk. It seemed authentic, as if she wasn't just in front of me because she was getting paid.

Still, opening up to her took some time. In the beginning, I refused to admit when I didn't understand something she told me.

"Yeah, I get it," I said automatically.

She narrowed her eyes. "Can you explain it to me?"

I avoided making eye contact and racked my brain for a description. I didn't have one. Instead of answering, I played with the book on my desk.

"Time out, Devin," she said, shutting the book and setting it aside. "Why did you tell me you understand when you don't?"

"Well, I thought ..."

"No, you didn't 'think' anything. You are far too bright for that. You have been conning people all your life, but you're not going to con me."

I slumped in my seat. Why wouldn't she just let me be?

"We only have fifty minutes together. I need you to answer me honestly when I ask you questions. Do you want to get better or do you not?"

I shifted around. Damn, she was persistent. My own teacher wouldn't stop class to make sure one trouble-maker followed along and understood anything. Why did this little white troll care so much?

"Are you prepared to tell your parents you're giving up? That's fine with me. There is a place for average people in the world."

Average people. My whole life, my parents had drilled into me that I wasn't average, that I was destined for something more, something great. Intuitively, my tutor had tapped into my desire not to be average. I had never heard talk like that from a teacher or from a woman other than my mother. I loved it.

One of the skills we practiced over and over was reading out loud. Working with her differed greatly from my regular classroom. Here, without other students to judge me and laugh at me, there was no social stigma; here, I had someone who cared how much progress I made. It was okay to show her my faults, even though I fought that vulnerability as hard as I could. I sat at a desk with *Little Women* open in front of me; she sat right next to me with the same book, following along without looking over my shoulder.

"After twenty minutes, everyone everyone ran—"

She put her hand on my arm when she heard the repetition. "Stop right there. Try that sentence again."

I tried it again, slowly. Every time I repeated myself, we would stop and go over that sentence a few times. During breaks, I played basketball for fifteen minutes while she went over my writing or looked for new assignments. It was unbelievable; I actually had fun in school!

"I want you to read the first sentence on the next page, but I want you to say it in your head before you read it out loud."

I concentrated on the words, thinking them out before I opened my mouth. I imagined the sound of the sentence in my head.

"Got it?"

"Yes."

"Okay, practice it in your head a couple of times, and then when you're ready, I want you to read it to me."

I sounded out every syllable in silence, then carefully put my voice into it.

"'I'm not Meg tonight, I'm 'a doll' who does all sorts of crazy things.'"

"Way to go!" she exclaimed when I finished. "Give me five." She held out her palm and I slapped it, grinning in spite of myself.

Her enthusiasm was infectious. I had never associated excitement with academia; to me, school was a sterile environment of frustration. In this room, however, studying and learning felt like scoring touchdowns on the field. She was more of a coach than my teacher, and my successes were her successes. That was the positive feedback I needed to forge ahead. The world told me to give up, to sit in the slow class and be one of the dumb kids. Now I had some tools in my belt to work with. Sounding the words out in my head became second nature.

I always felt good when I left our sessions, because I always felt as if I'd made progress. I felt more confident in school, too. Overall, my whole emotional temperament improved. I still tried to be a funny guy in class, but I wasn't seeking out attention as much. I started to enjoy learning; my tutor had found a way to ignite a little bit of the same fire I felt for sports. Within a few months, I was less apt to zone out in class. I stopped avoiding eye contact with my teacher. I even raised my hand to read aloud, which I never wanted to do before. That small action, raising my hand and seeking to engage with the world around me, was a milestone, a little victory to peel off some of the baggage I carried around every day.

I walked to the front of the room, my head held high and a library copy of *Sounder* clutched in my hand. The last time I'd read in front of the class, I skipped some words and the snickers and giggles bounced around the room like renegade ping-pong balls. This time, the words on the page marched across in straight lines of text. I took a deep breath and sounded them out in my head before I started speaking.

"'The boy was crying now. Not that there was any new or sudden sorrow. There just seemed to be nothing else to fill up the vast lostness of the moment.'"

Forty-five seconds later, it was all over. Elation set in. I had proved to myself and to others that I could do it, and I couldn't wait to tell my tutor.

I didn't say a word to Dad in the car on the way to my tutoring session, so I was bursting by the time we got there. She would understand. I ran to the room as fast as I could but tried to hide my excitement before I went in.

"How's it going this week?" she asked, as always.

"Good," I said, feigning nonchalance. "I volunteered to read out loud in front of the class today."

She waited for me to continue.

A wide smile stretched across my face. Quietly, I said,

"It was awesome."

Her face split into a beam of genuine happiness. "Congratulations, Devin! That's excellent!" She hugged me. I froze. I didn't push her away, but I didn't know what to do. I couldn't remember the last time I had been hugged. Was I supposed to squeeze back? As awkward as it was, for an affection-starved kid like me, one hug made a huge difference; she was truly proud of me.

"How did you feel about it?" she asked, pulling away.

"I was a little nervous," I admitted.

She smiled conspiratorially. "But you nailed it, didn't you?"

I grinned. "Yeah, I did."

I loved that she expected that from me. She understood my struggles and still thought I was bright and special. She made me see the possibilities that Dad always talked about. Maybe I *was* meant for bigger things, and reading was just a little bump in the road.

Mom asked a lot of questions when she picked me up from my tutoring sessions. She must have sensed the positive shift in my mood.

"How was your class today?" she asked as we pulled out of the parking lot. The clicking of the blinker filled the quiet moments before I answered.

"It was good."

"Do you like going?"

I shrugged. "Sure, I guess." I never told her how much I liked these sessions, but I didn't resist the same way I resisted all other academic-related subjects.

Mom turned her head to see if any cars were coming before she drove onto the street. "I talked to your tutor the other day. She said you're making great progress."

A smile threatened to break across my cheeks, so I bit my lip and stared out the window. Between feeling confident in myself and the acknowledgment from Mom, I felt like I was in a really good place. Success was about the process, not perfection. Just like a puzzle, the pieces began to fit together.

I worked with the tutor twice a week for nearly two years before our relationship ended. I didn't make a conscious decision on my own, but we had come to the end of the process naturally. School didn't feel as arduous, my grades improved, and I felt ready. She no longer gave me tips and strategies, but drilled me and helped me practice the tools I had already acquired. Our last day together was like the final spin around a dance floor. The music stopped. We both knew we had done what we were supposed to do. We celebrated the time we had and enjoyed ourselves up until the last note, and that was it.

All throughout the process of getting help with my formal education, Dad continued my alternative curriculum. We went to see the hookers on an inconsistent, but regular, basis. By now I loved riding down 14th Street. The interactions didn't change much, but every woman we talked to came from a different background, so we had similar conversations from a lot of different perspectives.

On the way home one night, Dad laughed and joked as usual. He'd gotten his hand job and was in a good mood. Halfway back to the apartment, he slammed on the brakes.

"Shit," he said.

The brakes squealed. I grabbed the door handle to keep from flying into the dashboard.

"What's wrong?" I asked.

Dad patted his pockets frantically. "She stole my wallet! That bitch stole my wallet!" He made a U-turn and raced back toward 14th. "You see, son? You can't trust anybody."

What did he expect? She was a hooker, after all. Ever the consummate educator, Dad lectured on the importance of watching my own back while we cruised up and down 14th looking for the pilfering prostitute. Even though we did at least ten passes of her corner, we never saw her again.

Each trip was a new expedition in social archeology, and I was the Indiana Jones of DC's dark side. I started paying attention to finer details—the girls' hair, their lips, or the way they smelled underneath the cloying scent of perfume. Occasionally, Dad would point one out and identify her as a drug addict.

"Look at her eyes. She's high right now." He rolled my window down and beckoned her to come closer. She approached, her steps listless and uncaring. Every curve of her body showed through her skintight dress. I looked carefully, trying to figure out the telltale signs of her love affair with drugs.

"Hey, baby," Dad said with a smile. "You better watch yourself walking around the street high all night."

The girl waved the back of her hand at us. "You don't know what you're talking about. I've been out here for years. I'll be fine." Even so, her eyes darted right and left. She was worried about either her pimp or the police.

Dad never seemed uncomfortable about the threat of police presence. Down in the bottom of the cesspool, there was comfort in knowing that everyone on the street was there for seedy purposes. Part of the intrigue of it was wondering how all these different people came to be a part of this bizarre night world. Especially when I saw girls who seemed lucid or articulate, I couldn't figure out how they ended up walking these corners. Beyond the Farrah Fawcett look-alike when I was younger, I never had the courage to ask.

When I was twelve, Dad surprised me with a trip to a massage parlor. My heart jackhammered as soon as Dad killed the engine in front of a large house. Most of the time, we just pulled over to the curb and he let the motor idle while we talked to the girls. I didn't know what to do. Dad opened the car door. I didn't want to act like a pansy, so I stepped out.

"We're just going to go inside for a few minutes," Dad said.

Inside, a handful of women lounged in a waiting area. The room was dark. Quiet music played from speakers that crackled softly with static. I stuck as close to the wall as I could, trying to blend into the wallpaper while Dad talked to one of the girls. No one came up to talk to me. That was fine. I avoided looking at anyone else.

Next thing I knew, Dad called me over.

"Hey, Devin," he said in a loud whisper.

Crossing that small hallway took ages, as though I had to drag my feet through two-foot-deep wet cement.

Dad put one arm around me and pointed at the girl

next to him. "This nice girl wants to talk to you. I'm going to wait out here while you two go back in that room and have a conversation."

"Huh." I didn't know what to say. For the first time, I regarded the girl. Dad told me her name, but I forgot it as soon as he said it. She didn't look like most of the women out on the street. She was *hot*. Her dress covered most of her body between her shoulders and knees, but it clung like wet silk in all the right places. Her brown hair shone in the dim light. When she smiled, I felt my anxiety abate a little. "Okay."

"I'll be right out here," Dad promised.

The girl took my hand and led me past a heavy curtain and into a small room. She hopped onto the edge of a short table in the middle of the room and patted the spot next to her.

I crossed my arms over my chest and stood just inside the curtain. Dad was within earshot, but that didn't make me any more comfortable.

She smiled again. "Your father is a little …"—she paused to find the right word—"*different*, isn't he?"

We both laughed. Her voice was mellow and sweet. *He is definitely different*, I thought.

"So, what do you want to talk about?" she asked. Her legs swung back and forth over the edge of the table. Her dress had crept up her thighs a few inches, exposing soft, gleaming skin. "You must have questions about something."

I could tell where the conversation was going, but I had no idea what to say. Silence seemed like it would be an offense, so I searched for the small talk I'd learned from watching my father interact with hookers.

"Where are you from?"

She smiled and avoided the question. "Do you like sports?"

Sports were safe. I could talk about sports. "I like the Redskins."

"Yeah? You know, you're going to be a lady-killer some day."

What was I supposed to say to that? I studied the carpet under my feet.

"What do you know about girls?"

I shrugged.

"You're such a cutie. You're going to have girls all over you."

My cheeks burned I was blushing so hard. If I opened my mouth I was going to stutter like an idiot, I knew it.

She reached out her hand. "Come over here."

I took a few steps forward, never taking my eyes off those slender hands. She threaded her fingers through mine and pulled me closer. We were so close now I could feel her breath against my face.

"Have you ever kissed a girl?"

"No." Her skin was soft, warm. Her touch sent electric tingles down my arm.

"Relax for a second. I'm not going to hurt you." She brought my hand up to her breast and ran my fingertips over her nipple.

My insides went crazy. I licked my lips, nerves and excitement fighting for dominance in my chest. Every few seconds, I let my eyes wander to hers, but I looked away as soon as I saw her looking back.

"Sweetie, you can look at me. It's okay." She let me get used to the sensation for a few minutes and then started giving me a tutorial. "This is my breast," she said. Clutching my hand tighter against her chest, she showed me how to play with her body. "Women like to be touched like this."

I had no way to explain what was happening to me; I was excited, nervous, and scared all at once. Thoughts raced through my mind, but I couldn't hold on to a single one long enough to figure out how I felt.

"Devin, I'm going to touch you now, okay? Don't get nervous." With one practiced motion, her fingers undid the button of my jeans. Her hands stroked me up and down. "Doesn't that feel good?"

By this time, I couldn't focus on anything she said. My body was on fire, my breath coming out in short bursts.

Her voice kept up a steady stream of soft murmurs. "Relax, honey, relax."

The whole experience seemed like twenty hours but in reality only took fifteen minutes. She walked out with me when she was finished and talked to my dad. Maybe he paid her; I couldn't concentrate on anything. I felt as if I had undergone some important rite of passage. I felt like a man.

In the car, I leaned back in my seat and pressed my forehead against the cool window. The nightlife raced past in a blur outside. My brain was going at warp speed, trying to make sense of what had just happened.

Dad didn't speak until we pulled into the parking lot outside the apartment. "How did everything go?"

"Great. She was really nice."

He turned to me, a serious expression on his face. "Don't tell your mom what happened tonight. She wouldn't understand. This is man stuff."

"Okay." No problem. This was far from anything I'd want to talk about with Mom.

"It's important that you understand the relationship between men and women. Although what you experienced might have felt great, you have to be careful because women can take advantage of you."

Like the hooker who stole your wallet? I didn't say it out loud.

"Don't put yourself in positions where you can be compromised because of that feeling. Understand?"

"Yeah, Pops. I understand." I truly did. I had no idea why Dad exposed me to all these experiences that no one else my age was going through, but I liked it. Every day was a new adventure, and even when it was scary, I felt safe because Dad was there with me.

CHAPTER 10

BANKING THE EMBERS

IN NINTH GRADE, MY PARENTS TRANSFERRED ME TO ST. JOHN'S COLLEGE HIGH SCHOOL, an independent

Catholic military preparatory school with a JROTC program. Every day I had to wear the Junior ROTC uniform: dark green pants, light green shirt, black shoes, belt, buckle, hat, and depending on the season, a black tie. The dark green jacket was optional during class hours but required for inspections. The jacket carried our identities at St. John's: a nametag told our superiors who we were, and the brass and accoutrements proclaimed our achievements.

What a pain. The jacket made me sweat. My shoes always had to be shined, my brass polished to a gleam. It wasn't just the uniform that had to be neat and pressed, either; there were rules about shaving and how long my hair could be. While in formation, we couldn't have anything bulky in our pockets, including our own hands, so we had to make sure our fingernails were clean at all times. I stood in ranks with my classmates while the officers drilled us on our appearance and the chain of command.

"Who's the commander in chief?" he barked at someone on the other end of the hallway.

I didn't hear the response. I squared my shoulders and kept my eyes forward as the sergeant progressed down the line. I recited the names of the secretary of defense and the Joint Chiefs of Staff in my head in case he asked me. He passed by so close I felt the brim of his hat brush my forehead. I didn't flinch but breathed a sigh of relief on the inside.

My parents were proud of that uniform; my dad had

been in the Air Force, and he got a kick out of seeing me in my Class As. They took pictures of me sitting, standing, smiling, not smiling. I hated it. Taking orders from others wasn't one of my fortes, unless there was a basketball court involved.

St. John's had a freshman team, a JV team, and a varsity team. Steve Grant coached the freshman team. He also served as the school's disciplinarian. Everyone knew Coach Grant. At six foot two, he was tough to miss in the hallways. He had curly brown hair cut to regulation length and a thick brown mustache. He played for the school basketball team back in his day and was notorious for his intensity. As part of his duties as head of discipline, he ran the combined study hall and detention session at the end of the school day. I sat at the back of the room with the rest of the team and avoided becoming a blip on his radar during detention. When the bell rang, we all headed to the gym to change for practice.

For practice, we wore standard basketball attire in the school colors. Our shorts were red, and the jerseys reversible: white on one side, red on the other.

"Listen up, men," he said at the start of my first practice. "This team is not about *me*—it's about us. This team is not about *you*—it's about us." He let those words sink in for a moment as he caught my eye. "Teamwork, effort, and commitment are what I expect every day. Warm-up is twenty laps. Go." The shrill cry of his whistle pierced the quiet spell that hung over us, and we made a mad dash for the court.

Coach Grant didn't accept less than our best.

Occasionally I came to practice feeling lazy or tired, and he noticed every time.

"Hughes!" His voice boomed across the gym.

I flinched. I'd been practicing halfhearted layups with some of the other guys and skipped my turn in line a couple of times.

"Hughes!" he shouted again as he jogged over.

I knew I was in for it. Reluctantly, I went to face him at center court. The floorboards vibrated under dribbled basketballs.

"Why are you wasting your time here?"

"I'm not. I'm doing my best."

He stomped his foot. "Your best? Can you look around at the rest of your team here and honestly tell me you're putting in as much work as everyone else?"

I looked around the gym. The rest of the team stared at me. A giant spotlight shone directly on me, singling me out among the group.

"Effort and commitment—if you can't give me that, you don't belong on this team. Get back in there and show me something."

Coach Grant and my tutor were both passionate and authentic; they spoke in plain English without a lot of double-talk. Every day they challenged me, and little by little through those interactions I came to trust them and their intentions. After a while, I started to buy into the messages that Coach Grant pushed on us, not only on the court but everything he did to develop his students as men of character. I gravitated toward that. The team came together and we put in a lot of hours having fun and working hard.

After practice, he pulled me aside to talk about my lack of effort; he wouldn't leave his players seething after a public confrontation. He and my dad coached from the same playbook in that way. He pushed us, yelled, screamed, threw his keys at the wall, but no matter how uncomfortable he made us in the moment, we could tell it came from a good place.

The passion he had for the team bled into all of us. I played with a few guys I went to middle school with, but I also made some new friends on that freshman team. Erik Harris, Eddie Reddick, Richard Washington, Robert Harris, Ernest Jackson, and I formed a tight nucleus. We watched the JV and varsity teams closely, measuring ourselves against the rich heritage of St. John's basketball. As the momentum of twenty-one wins carried us through to the championship against the other schools in our conference, we thought about how we could move up through the ranks together and leave our own stamp on the program. We won the championship.

That win started us all down a shared journey that was more than just building friendship—we knew we were building a legacy that would outlast all of us at the school. The six of us played all through the summer and got to know one another on a deeper level than we would have without basketball.

Rick Washington lived near my apartment. His basketball skills were only a little better than average, but he worked hard and was a good guy. Rick's dad was black, and his mom was Mexican. You could tell he was mixed, but he had dark skin. Like me, he identified more with his black roots, but where I was loud and funny, Rick was more introverted. We struck a nice balance when we hung out together.

"Hey man," Rick said when I walked out of the gym. After practice we could wear regular clothes, so we were both dressed in jeans and T-shirts, like normal kids.

"Did you book any last night?"

Rick grinned. "Nah, not last night. Let's go to the library and change that."

Booking was our code for picking up girls. Since we couldn't drive yet, we walked to the library or the mall to find and flirt with them. On the weekends, I'd go to his house or he would come over to our apartment complex and we'd hang out on the stoop. We sat out there for hours cracking on each other or running around with some of the other guys in my neighborhood.

A few times, Dad took a bunch of us down 14th Street. I knew what was coming, but my friends didn't know what to expect. Four of us crammed into the back of the Buick, our eyes shining with the reflected nightlife. We rolled the windows down and hooted and hollered all the way down the street.

Rick pointed out a small group of hookers ambling down the sidewalk.

"Hey, sexy mama!" one of the other guys yelled.

"Hey, hey, look at that girl," somebody else said, pointing. The woman's pants were so tight they looked painted on. Elbows flew in the backseat as all four of us tried to look out the passenger's-side window. Dad slowed the car to a crawl to let us have our fun.

"Pull your pants out of your ass!" we shouted.

We were clowns. We laughed so hard our stomachs hurt.

"This is crazy." All three of them kept repeating those words.

One of the guys leaned out the window a little to shout at another girl as we rolled past. "Hey, baby—"

Before he finished his thought, I noticed a man dressed like Dad's cousin Jackie standing ten yards behind the women. I yanked on the back of my friend's shirt. "That's her pimp!" I tried to push my way through the tangle of my friends' bodies to talk to Dad. "Drive, Dad, drive!"

The Buick rolled forward, but not fast enough. We all held our breath as the pimp ran forward. He held a glass bottle of booze by its long neck.

"Go, Dad, faster!" My heart palpitated with a mixture of fear and excitement. I felt the same emotions coming from all of my friends.

The pimp drew his arm back and let the bottle fly.

"Oh, man, we have to get out of here!"

The bottle slammed against the back window and bounced off onto the asphalt. Moments later, Dad turned down another street and we all erupted with relieved laughter. That pimp scared the crap out of all of us, but we loved every minute of it.

Outside of school, my parents granted me more autonomy; I'd been taking care of myself for years at this point, but now I felt even more disconnected from them. Drugs and disagreements fractured their relationship and built toward the breaking point we all knew was coming. The only time we spent together was the occasional meal, but the majority of the time we all just grabbed our food and dispersed to our corners. I didn't mind that we didn't do anything as a family. As a teenager, I wanted freedom.

When Rick came over to hang out at my place, I always met him outside on the stoop. My home life wasn't something I shared with anyone.

"Hey, man," Rick said as he walked up one day. "I have to call my dad and let him know I'm over here. Can we go up and use the phone?"

I couldn't say no, but that didn't stop me from trying to think of an excuse. My mind raced as we pushed through the front door of the building. The walk up the single flight of stairs felt like a death march. What would he think? I didn't know if any gods were listening, but I sent up a silent prayer. *Please don't let Mom be getting high in the living room.* Slowly, I pushed the door open and hoped that by some miracle the place would be clean.

I saw the apartment through Rick's eyes. The kitchen and dining room sat right inside the front door. As usual, both rooms were filthy. Paper clutter and fast-food trash covered the dining room table; it looked as if we never threw any garbage away. Rick tried to play it cool. He made his phone call quickly and then said, "I'm hungry. You mind if I grab something to eat?"

I shrugged. I wished I could make him close his eyes long enough to get to the oasis of my room, the only place in the apartment that was relatively neat and organized. I wanted him to know I didn't choose to live like this.

He picked up a banana from the kitchen counter.

"Whoa!" he yelled in surprise.

Three fat roaches skittered away, crawling toward the edge of the counter.

"Man, I am not eating that." He dropped the banana on the counter and wiped his hand on the front of his shirt. "I gotta get out of here."

My face burned, all my fears validated.

That was the last time I let anyone come upstairs. On top of the mess, Mom was a wildcard. I never knew what condition she would be in, and I hated how fat she'd gotten and how she carried herself. She looked sloppy, and when she wasn't high, she was irritable. At times it felt like Dad and I had to tiptoe around her. She always seemed on edge, and it didn't take much to light her fuse. Mom continued to verbally hammer Dad, telling him he wasn't worth shit and would never amount to anything. I hated listening to them bicker.

The drugs and alcohol exacerbated their problems, leading to explosive altercations. I tried to pull them apart and have side conversations with each of them, but neither of them owned their part in the problem. Dad blamed Mom, and she blamed him. Eventually, that led us to family counseling at Howard University.

Dad had been seeing psychiatrists and psychologists for many years. Until they dragged me in for an office visit, I didn't realize he'd been on just about every drug available to treat depression: lithium, Prozac, you name it, Dad had been on it at some point. At first, I tagged along to their counseling sessions and sat in the lobby while my parents went behind a closed door to work on their problems. Eventually, I got roped into talking to the guy myself.

Stan Ridley was a black psychologist who specialized in couples' issues. I walked into his office by myself and sat across a small table from him. My guard was up. No way would I let this guy see the ball of pain I'd pushed down deep inside.

"So, Devin, how do you feel about your parents arguing all the time?"

I considered my words carefully and let my eyes wander around the office. Framed certificates hung on one wall. A couple of half-dead plants sat in the windowsill. The doctor waited out my silence. He tapped one finger against his chin. His eyes narrowed when he looked at me. Everything about Dr. Ridley said he wanted to peel back my layers and expose the parts of me I didn't want anyone to see. I wasn't buying any of this. He wasn't going to make my parents stop fighting, he wasn't going to make them clean up the apartment, and he wasn't going to get them to stop doing drugs. What could he possibly do for me?

"Devin?" he repeated.

"Yeah, it's troubling, but I manage as best I can."

He put his elbows on the table and leaned forward. "How are you getting through that?"

I kept a straight face. "Through the grace of god."

"Why don't you tell me about some of your coping mechanisms."

"I've got a good support network with my friends at school," I said. Inside, I was having a different conversation: *I don't need your help.*

Those certificates on the wall weren't going to break me down. Soft words and disingenuous concern couldn't touch me. If he wanted to get through to me, he should've gotten in my face, used words that rocked me: *Devin, cut the bullshit.* He told my parents afterward that he could tell I was probably in some kind of emotional pain, but that I was a slick salesman so he couldn't identify how bad I was hurting.

Dr. Ridley treated the symptoms of my parents' problems but never touched the disease. After leaving his office, they would be okay for a couple of days. They'd walk out with smiles on their faces. What they really needed was to break their patterns of behavior. Both had addictive personalities and fell back into their old habits quickly. Dad went back to booze, Mom went back to pot, and they'd be in the exact same place before their next appointment with Dr. Ridley.

They continued this crazy charade for eight or nine months. What a joke. If they wanted to learn to dance, they had to practice in between their weekly one-hour lessons. They never practiced. They didn't want to admit failure, so they went to their therapy sessions and lied to Dr. Ridley.

Counseling became like story time. The doctor bought their lies with a smile on his face. I played along. I was great at pretending everything was cool. That's how I survived. I got in the habit of telling people what I thought they wanted to hear. Emotionally, I was a zombie. I lost sight of myself in the midst of the lies. I could only assume Mom and Dad did, too. They didn't know themselves, didn't know each other, and kept medicating themselves with their poisons of choice.

The apartment became a hotel for me—a place to put my head down at the end of the day, but not anywhere I wanted to spend time. My parents' relationship degenerated to the point that they separated again. They never told me anything. There was no "We're not getting along, and it doesn't make sense to keep living in the same house," or "We need a breath of fresh air." Dad found a girlfriend and moved out. The lease on the apartment ended and the rent went up, so Mom decided to move us across town. She didn't tell Dad.

I loved our new neighborhood. Our townhouse was much bigger than the old apartment, and it was clean and inviting. For the first time, I started to hope that we'd found the catalyst for changing our lives, to close one dysfunctional chapter and turn a new page. That hope was short lived.

CHAPTER 11

BONFIRE

WHEN MY PARENTS WERE HAVING ISSUES, DAD FOUND NEW GIRLFRIENDS QUICKLY. He maintained complete transparency, as always, and took me to meet them right away. I disliked them all on principle; I had enough dysfunction in my life, and these women added more. I could always tell when Dad had a new girlfriend. His mood lightened and he complained about Mom less.

The first girlfriend he took me to meet was Pam. On our first visit, Dad acted nonchalant, as though it was perfectly normal for a still-married man to bring his son to dinner at a new girlfriend's house.

"We're going to meet a friend of mine for dinner."

Friend. I knew what that meant.

He knocked on the door and smiled at me, his happy-go-lucky attitude in full force.

Pam opened the door and gave me a tight-lipped smile. "Hi, guys. Come on in."

It's Mom, was my first thought. *Only younger.* I couldn't help but notice the similarities between the two white women.

After giving my dad a quick hug, she ushered us through the door. "Come in, come in. Devin, the kids are watching TV in the living room. Why don't you go sit down with them?"

Dad followed her into the kitchen. I stayed rooted to the spot and took in my surroundings. The apartment was the same size as ours, but it was much cleaner and more orderly. This place had a sense of permanence about it. I didn't trust it. Resolving to keep my guard up, I shuffled out to the living room where Pam's kids sat on the couch. Neither of them looked up at me, so I didn't bother talking to them. I sat on the floor in front of the couch and we all stared at the TV in mutinous silence.

After dinner, we resumed our posts in the living room. Pam came to sit on the floor next to me.

"So, Devin, your dad tells me you're a really good basketball player."

"I do all right."

"That's awesome." The laugh track of the sitcom sounded forced in the silence that followed. She tried again. "I hear you're doing well in school."

"Yeah, I guess."

A few other failed attempts at establishing a connection later, she peeled herself off the floor and went to sit with my father. They held hands and laughed softly. I couldn't look away, but I didn't want to see. I didn't want to be here, but I was afraid to leave. Who else would make sure nothing else happened between them? I understood that Pam gave Dad something he was missing at home, but I hated that he needed it. I sat there and watched what could have been a good family life. This was the interaction that I wanted within my own family unit. Dad might as well have pulled off the emotional Band-Aid, ripped off the scab, and then kicked me in the back of the head. My heart screamed, but no one could hear it.

On our way home, Dad turned to me and said, "Look, I'm sharing something with you that is just between us. Pam is a nice girl. You're grown up, and I'm trusting you not to say anything about this to your mother."

I nodded reluctantly.

"I still love your mom, you know that, right?"

"I guess so."

"I love her more than I've ever loved anything in my life, but I'm having a hard time connecting with her."

I wasn't flattered by Dad's trust, but I kept his secret. Mom didn't know for a long time that Dad was seeing other women. Maybe she did know and was in denial. I wanted to tell her, but couldn't. There had always been a distance between the two of us, and keeping Dad's secrets widened the gulf. I was perpetually torn between my parents, wrestling with guilt and obligation. I retreated into myself and didn't tell either of them how much it hurt. A lump formed in my throat at this expression of raw pain from my father.

True to form, Dad went through relationships the way he went through religions. At the first sign of dissatisfaction, he became disillusioned and moved on to the next one. He did still love Mom, and he couldn't heal the emotional wounds between them outside our home. When they were separated, his emotions tipped rapidly from one side to the other, his moods oscillating from high to low at the slightest provocation.

Dad was always quick to fight, especially if he thought he was being disrespected. Once, Dad and I went to watch a football game at my high school. From the top of the stairway leading to the bleachers, we looked over the brightly lit field with all its rushing players. As we made our way toward our seats, a man muttered something to my father in passing. It sounded like "You need to move—get out of the way."

The man was white, and Dad assumed his comment was not just rude but racist. As if by instinct, Dad launched at the man, chasing him off the stairway and into the parking lot. I ran after them, humiliated as Dad tried to kick the guy in the ass—a move meant to be more demeaning than painful. At five foot eleven and one hundred and sixty pounds, Dad wasn't big, but he had no fear in situations like this.

Mom also had her share of extramarital relationships, but she didn't throw them in my face. Within three months of moving into the new townhouse, I woke up to faint noises coming from the living room in the middle of the night. I crept down the stairs quietly, a private eye on a reconnaissance mission. I peeked into the room. Mom sat on the floor with a black man I didn't recognize. They sat facing each other, their knees touching. Both of them looked relaxed. They passed a glass pipe back and forth, the flick of the lighter and their breathing the only sound. The stench of marijuana smoke filled my nostrils, but that wasn't what made me sick to my stomach—it was their ease. *Abort, abort!* the warning sirens in my head screamed. I retreated to my bedroom as fast as I could without alerting them to my presence. I crawled into bed, pulled the covers over my head, and tried to shut out what I'd just seen.

A few days after that, Dad showed up at the front door. It was three-thirty in the afternoon, and Mom had implored me not to let him in under any circumstance; he was on a bad streak with his bipolar disorder. She was still at work, and his fists banged against the door.

"Let me in, Devin!" he yelled. "Just let me in the damn house!"

I was nervous. Scared. Could the neighbors hear us?

The door rattled and shook under his pounding. It could break at any minute. I hovered indecisively on the other side of the door.

The noise stopped. As if he'd taken a deep breath, my father appealed to me in a softer voice. "I know your mom is seeing someone else. I just need to come in for a second. Let me in. I won't do anything. I just want to come in and grab a couple of things. I just want to talk."

I didn't want to let him in; Mom had told me not to, and I didn't know whether he was taking his lithium. At the same time, he sounded so weak and distressed that I felt sorry for him.

I opened the door. Dad charged in, the proverbial bull in the china shop. Rage poured off him in waves, complete and absolute.

"Where is your mom?"

"She's at work."

He started a quick, purposeful pace up to Mom's bedroom, muttering to himself. "Your damn mom. I try my best."

I kept a careful distance as he came out of her room with an armload of her clothes. The stairs creaked under his feet as he hustled down.

"I try my best and this is how she treats me." He yanked open the sliding glass door to the backyard and stomped outside. He dropped the clothing in a heap on the grass. Moments later, the pile smoldered and caught fire. The fabric of Mom's blouses, skirts, and pants blackened as Dad returned to Mom's room for another load, carrying on his half-muttered diatribe all the way. He must have made twenty trips.

The kitchen window overlooked the backyard, and I watched my mom's clothes go up in flames. Every time I heard the stairs creak under his weight, I cringed. When would this end? When would he be satisfied? *Stop!* I wanted to yell, but I didn't know what else he would do. It was the first time I had ever been scared of my father, and I didn't want to get in his way.

The battle between confronting him and staying out of his warpath raged inside me. I was also afraid to call my mom and tell her I had let him in the house. I didn't know how to tell her she was right, that I was sorry, that he was out of control and all her clothes were gone.

During one of Dad's trips up the stairs, I saw that the last armload he had dropped hadn't caught fire yet. I felt as though I needed to save something—I couldn't stand the thought of Mom coming home to nothing. I raced out the back door, grabbed whatever I could and threw it over the fence into our neighbors' yard. Those few outfits would be wet and dirty, but at least we could clean them. I didn't even see what I had grabbed; I didn't want him to catch me.

Even though I was afraid of my father, I also felt sorry for him. He was clearly in a lot of pain for which he had no other outlet, so we were both helpless in a way. The man walking through the house was so pitiful and raw, his emotional act so symbolic, his rage so primal, that I couldn't bring myself to interfere.

The bonfire seemed as though it would never end, but my father was only there for an hour. When the constant creak of the stairs waned, he stood before me in eerie silence. I didn't make eye contact. There was nothing to say. He walked out, leaving me behind with smoke rising from the backyard.

After he left, I tried to salvage whatever I could. I ran from the kitchen to the yard carrying pitchers of water like a crazy member of a nineteenth-century fire brigade and tried to put out the flames. I waited at least half an hour before I called Mom to let her know what had happened. Guilt gnawed at me as I dialed her number.

"Hello?"

"Mom, I'm sorry." Tears poured down my face. "I'm sorry, I'm so sorry."

"Devin, what's going on?"

For the first two minutes of the call, I couldn't do anything but cry and apologize. At first she seemed upset, but she switched to concern for me quickly.

"Don't worry about the clothes. We can figure that out. Are you hurt?"

"No."

"Is the fire still going?" She tried to keep me calm.

By that time, someone must have reported the smoke to the fire department, because I could hear sirens. I panicked. Mom was a disaster—she might have drug paraphernalia, or something else that would embarrass us, lying around. Whatever she might have, I had to find it before anyone else did.

I raced around the house, searching for bongs, pipes, drugs, and packaging. Anything I found, I hid under dirty clothes in Mom's closet. I was also hyperaware that the house was filthy; the neatness of a new house hadn't lasted long. I didn't want people to judge us as white trash, so amidst all the chaos, I started cleaning up, shoving clothes into closets, sweeping the floors, and keeping my eyes open for drug paraphernalia.

When Mom got home from work, police officers and firefighters filled the house. They followed Dad's path between her room and the charred pile of clothes outside, asking her questions I couldn't quite make out. Mom was embarrassed and tried to play it off as if it weren't a big deal.

"Are you sure you don't want to press charges?" one of the officers asked on his way out the door.

"Oh, no," Mom replied with a soft smile. "He's just gone off his medication, and that causes erratic behavior sometimes. Everything will be fine when he adjusts."

The cop handed her a card. "In case you change your mind. Have a good night, ma'am."

"Thank you, officer." Mom closed the door behind them and sagged against the wall. The fake smile she'd plastered on for the police melted from her face.

We sank down on separate couches in the living room. We were both distraught but didn't know how to comfort each other. She wept at the trauma—the violation—of coming home to all her clothes destroyed by my out-of-control father. I cried because I had let her down and because, for the first time, I had seen my father break.

In the end, Mom and I hauled a bunch of garbage bags out to the backyard and filled them with her ruined clothes. I remembered the few outfits I had rescued from the fire, and I ran into the neighbors' yard to retrieve them. I offered them to her, but I hadn't really saved them; the smoke damage was too bad.

My mom was angry, but she didn't blame my father.

"He's a sick man," she said, wiping her eyes. "He needs help. He was out of control, but he is still your father. He still means well."

Somehow, I couldn't pass judgment on him, either. I still loved him unconditionally. I just felt that he was flawed, or that he was a victim. His behavior was so erratic at times that we were both inured to it, even expected it. He was manic-depressive, an alcoholic and drug addict, and watching his family implode must have been heartbreaking. Looking at him through those lenses, I could see that he loved my mom but couldn't figure out how to put together the pieces of this puzzle. He just needed the pain to go away somehow.

Later that evening, I could hear Mom crying behind her closed bedroom door. I stood in the hallway and listened, my ear pressed against the wood. I wanted to knock but didn't know what to say, and I didn't dare go inside. A terrible feeling of guilt ate at me. At the same time, I wanted my father to be in a better place. Again, I felt torn between my parents and isolated from both of them. After listening to my mother cry, I compartmentalized the experience and forced it to the back of my mind.

The next day, it was almost as if it never happened. Mom put on a happy face. So did I; this townhouse was our chance to start fresh, and we clung to that belief. We never talked about it as a family. Beyond crying together, Mom and I didn't discuss why my father would do something like this; she put on her emotional windshield wipers and moved forward. In some ways, we threw out the entire experience along with my mom's ruined clothes, and only the smell of smoke lingered in my memory.

CHAPTER 12

SWEEPING THE ASHES

AFTER THE INSANITY OF THE BONFIRE, LIFE AT THE TOWN-HOUSE BECAME ROUTINE: ignore, rationalize, discount, and move forward. I tried to move on, but that was the first time I'd ever feared my father. Mom and I assumed Dad had gone off his medications, leading to the outburst, but how did we know whether he would start taking them again? How did I know this wasn't the first in a cascade of increasingly bad episodes? I didn't have much time to dwell on it; school, homework, and practice demanded my attention.

A week after the incident, Dad picked me up for the weekend.

"Hey," he called from the driver's-side window. "What do you say we go get something to eat?"

I couldn't say no. When I got into the car, I fidgeted constantly. I didn't know if I should bring up the fire or not; I didn't want to talk about it, but it felt strange not to address it.

Luckily, Dad threw it into the ring right away. "If your mother would get her head on straight, I wouldn't feel the need to do things like that."

I didn't have an answer for that. He was blaming *Mom* for what he had done? He wasn't going to take *any* responsibility? The streets of Silver Spring passed by outside. We drove in silence for ten minutes before he spoke again.

"It was stupid of me. I was out of control."

You think? I mentally rolled my eyes.

"I've never loved anyone as much as I love your mother, and I've been struggling with my medication and couldn't keep my emotions in check." He looked away from the road for a moment to gauge my reaction. "You have to keep your emotions under control."

I felt like Stan Ridley was sitting in the car with us, asking me how this made me feel. *Shut up, please just shut up.* I wanted him to stop talking. The quicker we could not-talk about it, the quicker I could flush it down the emotional toilet.

"So what did your mom say? Was she upset?"

"I guess." I tried not to flinch when he looked at me again.

"I gave her some money to buy new clothes. Did she tell you that?"

"No, Pops." Mom and I hadn't discussed the fire since the night we both cried on the couches.

"Does she ever say she wants to get back together? Does she know how much I love her?"

I sighed. "I know she loves you, but to be honest we don't talk about it. You probably need to bring it up with her."

"She doesn't want to talk to me right now."

Well, no shit. What do you expect? In the car with him, I felt like the adult. How did I get to be a marriage counselor? I wanted to be a teenager; teenagers didn't have to worry about managing relationships like this.

A flood of relief washed over me as we pulled into the parking lot of the restaurant. Once we got out of the car, we moved forward and talked about school, the A&P, and other neutral topics. In a way, I was disappointed; Dad hadn't even apologized for sabotaging the home team. What did that mean for his constant mantra: *you can't trust anyone but your mom, me, and the man in the mirror?*

As we ate, I realized that it wasn't just at home that Dad was going out of control. Work for him had always been a struggle because of the rampant racism, but the way he reacted to his boss's demands didn't help matters. I couldn't believe some of the stories he told me.

He started to relate a recent incident as we waited for our pizza to arrive. "One of the managers gave me a trash bag to throw away the other day."

"Since when are you the trash guy?"

"Right? So I look inside, and this bag is full to the top with steak and prime rib—some real nice cuts of meat." He paused to drink some soda. "So it occurs to me they're trying to set me up. They're going to imply that I put this meat in the bag and I was going to try to steal it by hiding it in a trash can."

"That's ridiculous! What did you do?"

"I went right back to the manager and said, 'Man, you must think I'm batshit crazy if you're going to set me up like that,' and I dropped it on the floor and left." Dad was in his element, gesturing with his arms and drawing attention while he talked.

"Did they make you put the meat back on the shelves?"

"I walked out of that office without looking back. This isn't the South. I'm not their slave."

"Do they do that kind of stuff to the other black workers?"

"Nah, I'm the one they're after because I won't be quiet when I see injustice. Everyone else is scared to talk back."

I told Mom some of the stories about his ordeals at work. She called his doctor and straightened out the situation with his medications, but it was a while before I felt comfortable being around Dad again.

I needed an escape from the mess at home. Basketball provided the physical outlet, and it helped my friends and me in our pursuit of girls. To us, it didn't matter who they were; it was about the thrill of the chase, the ego boost, and hanging out with friends.

St. John's was an all-boys school, so we looked for girls everywhere outside those walls. Parties and the mall were two obvious sources, but the greatest untapped resource was the public library. Where else could teenage boys get some homework done, socialize, and pick up girls all in one place? And what parents would argue with their kid about going to the library?

Despite what my friends told their parents, the main reason we went to the library was for socializing. Every day there were new people sitting at the tables, so every trip was unpredictable. We camped out far from the entrance and the shushing librarians. We had no interest in the people who were there just to loan and return books; we went after the ones who lingered.

"Hey, check her out," Rick whispered. He nodded his head toward a girl about our age a few tables away. She had a book open in front of her, but she looked up every couple of minutes and never turned a page.

"You going to talk to her or are you just going to look at her?" I asked.

"I'm keeping my options open." He grinned.

"Then I'm going in." I slid my chair back. Game on.

The self-confidence I picked up on the court gave me a natural swagger. I walked past her table and into the stacks. For a moment, I stood behind the first shelf and watched her over the top of the books. Then I grabbed a random book in front of me and pretended to be on my way back to the table where Rick sat watching me. Timing was key. I walked slowly until she looked up again and I caught her eye.

"What's up, girl?"

"Not much."

"What are you working on?" I asked as I slid into a chair across from her.

Her eyes crinkled at the corners, amused. "Studying."

"Yeah? Looks to me like you want a distraction."

"Says who?" She leaned back in her chair and crossed her arms over her chest.

"Says me." I smiled at the challenge; I could get the girls who played hard to get. I looked over my shoulder at Rick. He was laughing at me. "Come on, what are you studying? Maybe I can help you."

"You don't look like much of a studier."

"Hey, just because I'm an athlete doesn't mean I don't read. I'm at a library, aren't I?" The library was genius. We could always lead with the good-boy image.

"So, you play sports?"

"I play basketball at St. John's." I caught an interested twinkle in her eye.

"Are you any good?"

"Come see me play and you'll find out."

"Maybe I will."

I looked back at Rick and grinned. He rolled his eyes.

I chatted with the girl until I talked her into letting me walk her home. I never asked whether she already had a boyfriend. If she did, she wouldn't be accepting a walk home with me. Besides, I was better than any other boy she might have waiting in the wings.

That same line of thought got me into trouble a few times. I didn't do drugs, didn't drink, and didn't fall into some of the dangerous circles that guys from my neighborhood fell into; girls were the only thing that got me into trouble. Before Mom moved us out of the apartment, I'd been seeing a girl from the neighborhood. When we started hanging out, I had no idea she had a boyfriend. She never told me, even after we kissed. I found out the next day when I went downstairs and saw five guys waiting to jump me on the front steps. I stayed inside until they lost interest.

A few months later, I found myself in a similar situation caused by a girl named Wilma. We saw each other for a few months, had some fun. After we broke up, I heard she had an axe to grind; she ground that axe with anyone who would listen, but most of all with the ex-boyfriend she started seeing again.

One Saturday afternoon, Rick and I were on our way home after a football game. A few blocks down the way, we realized we were being followed. A group of six guys hung back a block or two, but as we distanced ourselves from the school football field, they drew closer. Rick threw a quick glance over his shoulder.

"They're getting closer," he said. "What should we do?"

"Walk faster." My nerves buzzed.

We picked up our pace, but the guys quickly surrounded me and elbowed Rick to the side. I tried to keep my cool. Head forward, eyes straight ahead. Keep walking. One of them emerged from the pack and walked backwards to face me. I'd seen him hanging out with Wilma recently. He was tall, muscular. I didn't want to fight him or his five friends.

"I hear you think you're a ladies' man," the leader said, jabbing a finger at my chest.

"What are you talking about?" Pleading ignorance seemed the safest option.

His eyes narrowed. "Don't play with me. You think you can do whatever you want with other people's girlfriends?"

The circle contracted around me. There were maybe twelve feet of space between the guys on all sides. My stomach flip-flopped. I tried to find Rick, but I couldn't see him. Not that it would do any good if I could—we were sorely outnumbered. I had to defuse this bomb, quickly.

"I don't know what you're talking about. I don't even know who you guys are." I put my hands out, palms up.

"Don't lie to me, player." Spit flew from his mouth on the word *player*. The muscles in his arm contracted and relaxed as he squeezed his hands into fists.

"Seriously, I would never do something like that." That part was true. Chasing girls was just a game; I never went after someone else's girlfriend in a malicious way.

"That's not what Wilma tells me."

A dozen quick retorts flashed through my brain, but I didn't want my mouth getting me into trouble my fists couldn't get me out of. I choked back the sarcasm and kept my lips pressed together.

"She tells me you think you're real smooth."

Irritated now, I looked him in the face. I assumed the same bravado I saw Dad use with the prisoners we drove to work-release. But I'd failed to see a crack coming up in the sidewalk and suddenly tripped. Anger flared as I felt the skin of my palms scrape against the pavement. The circle instantly contracted around me. *Get up!* Adrenaline shot through my veins and propelled me to my feet. Who knew what would happen if I stayed on the ground?

"Can't be all that smooth if you're falling on your face," he taunted.

"Shut the hell up," I said quietly. My hands hurt and there were too many of them for me to fight, even if I wanted to. "I haven't done anything, so leave me alone."

They followed me a few more blocks. I hung on to my false bravado until they lost interest in trying to provoke me. From that point onward, I tried to make sure I never put myself in a position like that again.

The crowd I hung out with at the townhouse wasn't all that different from the one I'd run with back at our old apartment. More of my social circle lived in houses than apartments, but we were all still from the same socioeconomic background. The street served as our primary hangout. Drugs and alcohol were constant topics of conversation from the guys in the neighborhood, but no one in my inner circle did drugs, so I never felt much peer pressure. Drugs would have been easy to get, but to me they were taboo. For one, I thought drugs were nothing more than a way for the mentally weak to escape their problems. The other reason I avoided them was that I saw the way people acted when they were on drugs. Drugs made them silly and vulnerable. I didn't feel comfortable when I couldn't be on my A-game.

As usual, my new social circle was predominantly black, which helped me get attention from girls. I stood out from the crowd. Every time I met new girls, my looks came up in conversation.

"You have such pretty eyes," said the shorter of the girls Rick and I walked home from the library.

Her friend nodded in agreement. "You're going to make great babies because of your light skin."

We chatted for a few minutes before saying good-bye to the girls and heading home.

"Man, you can do whatever you want. The girls love you," Rick said enviously.

I shrugged noncommittally. I just used what I had to my advantage. In the black community, the darkness of your skin was another factor to consider in social inter-actions. People made fun of you if you were especially dark: "You're *African* black," you might hear. "You're purple."

I was on the other end of the light–dark spectrum. It felt weird to be primarily around black people and hear them make fun of white people. Whites were terminally uncool, corny, nonathletic dorks. It was like the never-ending debate of Magic Johnson versus Larry Bird, black versus white; everyone I knew rooted along the race line, and I was neither one nor the other. Finding my own identity felt impossible.

By the same token, though, I felt at liberty to jump in the pool and make fun of both sides. Anyone I thought was messing around with me felt the razor edge of my tongue. I cut so quick it would take them a while to figure out they were bleeding, and by that time everyone was laughing. Yo-mama battles were one of my specialties.

"Yo mama's so fat, her butt cheeks clap when she walks."

"Yo mama's so fat she needs a kickstand to stand up."

To me, it was better to go on the offensive than to let someone else kick me around. I thought it was funny; it wasn't to be hurtful. I never wanted to hurt people's feelings, though I assume I did.

I laughed and joked my way through the first year of high school but hit a brick wall when it came to geometry. The shapes and letters on the page all ran together. How was I supposed to know what angle A had to do with angle B? I didn't get it, and the teacher could tell, but he didn't help. This time I knew better than to shut down and resign myself to the dumb group.

I took a handful of homework assignments I had failed and put them down on the table. Mom was busy unpacking a McDonald's dinner amidst the garbage.

"What are those?" she asked, gesturing at the papers with a French fry.

"Geometry."

"Let me see." She licked the salt off her fingers and wiped her hand on the side of her pants leg.

I handed them to her. Mom looked at the angry Fs scrawled at the top of the papers. She glanced at me and then put the assignments down on the table. With a long sigh, she let herself sink into a chair. The fast-food bag rustled as she dug around for my double cheeseburger. She passed me a Styrofoam burger box in silence and pointed at the chair next to her.

"Do we need to have a talk?"

I shook my head and screwed up the courage to admit I needed help. "I just don't understand it."

Mom lit a cigarette and scanned the papers again. Smoke snuck out between her lips as she sat in thought. "Well, we'll just have to see what we can do about that."

True to her word, she found me a tutor right away. I have no idea where she found this woman, but she was fantastic. She was a stay-at-home mom of two young children. Once a week, I went to their house with my homework, and she methodically stepped through the lesson plan with me at their dining room table.

At first, all I could think when I met this woman was that she was hot—white, about five foot eight, and thin, with a friendly, warm smile. I could tell she cared about her health and appearance.

"Do you exercise a lot?" I asked, thinking about Mom's habit of coming home with fast food and going straight to bed.

"All the time. I have to if I want to keep up with my kids."

"Do you smoke?"

"Absolutely not. I would never do that."

My heart sank. Mom wasn't going to quit smoking or start working out; no matter how much I wished it, she wouldn't be like this woman.

My tutor tapped her pencil on my book. "Let's get back to math, okay? Why don't you show me your work for the first problem?"

Once my infatuation with the tutor settled, I felt awestruck by the house: it was neat and tidy. Books sat on shelves, not all over the table. A couple of cushions were nestled in the corners of the couch. The carpet and floors were all clean. Everything had a place. I felt as if I could breathe, relax my constant guard in a place of quiet refuge.

Although Mom found the tutor for me, Dad was the one who dropped me off and picked me up every day. When he came knocking on the door, she jumped up from her chair.

"You keep working on that last proof," she told me. "You'll get it."

"I doubt it," I mumbled under my breath. The eraser of my pencil was worn down to the metal already, and I didn't feel any closer to solving the puzzle.

She left the room. I heard her greet Dad, and his voice rumbled in response. Their words were muffled, but her tone was bright and chipper.

The more I stared at my paper, the less sense the problem made. The shapes and numbers all ran together into one big mess. I couldn't do it. I jammed the paper into my textbook and threw it in my backpack.

"There he is!" My tutor beamed as I walked out of the dining room. She put a hand on my shoulder to stop me from walking out the door. "Mr. Hughes, Devin is doing so great. He has come so far so fast that he won't need me for long."

"Is that so?" Dad grinned at me. My tutor's enthusiasm was infectious.

Both of them were so excited that I couldn't admit I hadn't finished the last problem. "Yeah, I'm doing great."

I failed the next quiz. On the way to my tutor's house the following week, I dreaded having to tell her. She saw it on my face as soon as she opened the door.

"That doesn't look like good news," she said.

I took a deep breath. "I didn't understand what we did last week."

"Is that all?" She smiled. "We can fix that."

Some of the tension I'd felt on the way over melted away. Between her positive attitude and the refreshing serenity of the clean house, I could almost believe her. Until we sat down at the table and I pulled out my crinkled sheet of notebook paper. Graphite lines covered the page, but it looked like secret code.

"Why don't you show me where you got stuck and we'll go from there?"

I stared at the paper. A triangle ringed in letters and two extra lines stared back. *Given that QR is congruent to ST and UR is congruent to US, prove that angle QUR is equal to angle TUR.* I tried to remember what my teacher had said, but my mind drew a blank. I started to daydream about living in this house, with a mom like this woman.

"Devin?"

"What?"

"Can you show me where you got stuck?"

I threw my pencil down and shoved the book aside.

"I don't get any of it!" The pencil rolled off the end of the table.

She ignored my outburst. "Then we'll start from the top. Pick up your pencil and I'll show you how I would attack the problem."

"It's too hard."

"No, it's hard right now. Soon it'll be easy. You'll see."

She walked through that problem step by step, drilling each item I had to list in the proof. Little by little, the pieces of the puzzle fell into place. After she finished the problem, she made me do it on my own. My memorization skills came in handy.

"Good job!" she exclaimed after I repeated the steps back to her. "Now, you try this one on your own."

Dejection set in; memorization wouldn't help with a new problem. My brain started to object. *I can't do this.* I stared at the paper until the lines blurred together.

"Devin?" She touched my shoulder. "Don't try to solve the whole thing at once. Just start with the first obvious thing you see from the given statements."

If I'd gripped my pencil any tighter, it would have snapped. I stared at the two triangles I was supposed to prove were congruent. One of the things she'd told me about the sides opposite the angles flashed through my mind.

"If this angle is the same as that one, then these two sides are the same, too?" I guessed.

"Exactly! That's a great start!"

She was a godsend for my math grades. She made me see that being bad at math was not a lifetime affliction. All I needed were a few shortcuts and some repetition. Once I became comfortable with the concepts, I felt like it was okay to get a problem wrong as long as I learned from it. She created an open, safe environment where I learned life lessons along with mathematics.

"Honey, I'm home," her husband's voice drifted into the dining room from the entryway.

"We're in here," she called back.

Moments later, a tall white man with a mustache came through the doorway. He carried a small briefcase and wore a suit and tie. He hugged and kissed his wife while I sat and watched like I was a live studio audience. A pang of covetousness echoed in my chest. These two loved each other.

"You must be Devin," he said to me, clapping a hand on my shoulder. I turned toward him, and he immediately grabbed my hand in a firm handshake. "I hear you're doing great work. Keep it up." He winked at his wife, making her blush.

"Daddy!" Their children ran into the room and leapt into his arms.

"Hey, guys, let's go to the kitchen and let Mom finish up. Who wants to help me make dinner?" Kids in tow, he walked out of the dining room. I caught glimpses of him in the next room. He tied an apron around his waist and opened the fridge.

Had I inadvertently wandered onto the set of *Leave It to Beaver*? How was this family so put together? Why couldn't my family be like this? I wondered what it would be like to live here. I bet she made pancakes in the morning and they all ate together at the table. The dad would read interesting parts of the paper out loud while she poured the kids juice, and the whole house would smell like coffee and hot sizzling bacon. Then he'd kiss her good-bye and she'd clean the kitchen before corralling the kids for baths and story time. Did these kids know how lucky they were? No. How could they possibly know? They hadn't experienced the contrast yet.

Every time we finished working, I hoped she would invite me to stay for dinner; I wanted to be a part of this house, this family, for as long as I could, but I was scared to ask. Asking to stay meant that I didn't want to leave. It felt too vulnerable to admit that, even indirectly, so I just took my time putting my things away. I snuck glances at her as I packed up, willing myself to at least say the chicken baking in the oven smelled good, but even that was too much for me.

I never stayed for dinner. In a way, I was glad they never invited me. What if I couldn't let it go afterward— the mom I craved but never had at home? The family that cooked and laughed together? Maybe it was better never to experience that joy than to know I had to leave it behind. All the same, the contrast between their life and mine was so powerful I resolved to build this kind of experience, not just for myself, but for the next generation of those who would carry my name. If I couldn't have it now, maybe I could find a way to work toward it.

"How long have you been together?" I asked her one day after her husband came in and they went through the same hug-and-kiss routine.

"We met in college. We dated for a very long time."

College. I hadn't given college much thought, but if that was part of the process to get to a place like this, maybe that was my next step. "What did you study?"

"I majored in math," she said with a smile as she wiggled the book in front of me. "And my husband studied business."

This is what I want. Sitting there, watching this family interact, I made a conscious decision: I would settle for nothing less than the warmth and functionality of *this* life, *these* people. The only problem was, aside from the vague notion of college, I had no idea where to find the cookbook with the secret recipe for success.

CHAPTER 13

YELLOW BRICK ROAD

FOR FOUR MONTHS, MOM CHECKED IN WITH DAD'S DOCTORS AND MADE SURE HE STAYED ON HIS MEDICATION.

They circled each other like a couple of prizefighters. By this time they'd had so many altercations, taken so many blows to the head, that neither had the energy to fight the other anymore.

Mom often mentioned how well Dad was doing on his medication. "A young man like you needs a father figure in your life," she told me as she hustled out the door on the way to work. She still had a soft spot for him.

I wasn't surprised when Dad showed up on the doorstep that afternoon.

"I told your mom I was sorry," he said. He didn't come in right away. "We both just want to get through the day-to-day, and I want to be a part of your life."

He seemed more lucid than last time I'd seen him. The crazy light had gone from his eyes. Lithium had a balancing effect on him. I stepped back and let him in the house. Just like that, we were a family of three again. My happiness was tinged with skepticism. Who knew how long this cease-fire would last?

When I was young, my parents had fought physically and regularly. They'd gotten all that out of their system; now they resorted to drugs. Mom had moved on from pot to "lovely"—marijuana laced with PCP—and now she smoked crack. I didn't realize it at the time—to me, drugs were drugs. They kept the paraphernalia out of the living room and kitchen, but their bedroom was littered with pipes of all shapes and sizes. I never found needles, though, so I knew they weren't on heroin. Given our financial situation, pure cocaine was out of their reach, but I knew people in their social circle were doing it.

Drugs were only a small part of my parents' decline. In the mornings, I saw Mom come in from work while I ate cereal. She was never a thin woman, but she gained even more weight on her steady diet of cigarettes, booze, and fast food. She didn't seem to care.

"Good morning," I said as she trudged through the front door.

She barely acknowledged me. Her hair looked matted on one side of her head. Makeup clumped her eyelashes together and clung in greasy lines to the folds in her skin.

"How was work?"

"Fine," she muttered. She opened the refrigerator, her bulk silhouetted in the weak glow of the fridge light. Can of Coke in hand, she walked past me to go upstairs. I caught the scent of unwashed hair and stale smoke trailing the air behind her.

I wrinkled my nose. Not cleaning the house was one thing. Not caring about personal hygiene was another.

She maintained her crazy work schedule all throughout my high school career. Outside of the house she was a fully functional member of society, but it was like she was caught on a high-speed train; once she started down the path of drugs and alcohol, the only option she had was to continue down the tracks and see where it led her.

Dad got caught on the same train.

The hallway floors creaked when you walked on them, and my father's measured footsteps became a familiar sound late at night. One night, I ran into him on my way back from the bathroom. It was after ten thirty.

"Hey, Dad."

He jumped a little, startled. "Oh, hey. You go to bed. I got to go run an errand."

I knew what that meant. I didn't know where they got the drugs, but it must have been somewhere in the city; that was one place Dad never set out to take me on an adventure, at least not explicitly. I resumed my policy of avoidance. The townhouse took on the same motel-like quality the old apartment had; I came in when I needed a place to sleep, and stayed away as much as I could otherwise.

We were driving around in the car one afternoon when the realization first dawned on me that although Dad never took me to meet his dealer, he wasn't actively keeping me away from that part of his life, either. The neighborhood outside the car looked tough, even by our standards. Houses in various stages of wear and tear crowded together on unkempt lawns. Junk and forgotten children's toys cluttered the front yards. Dad slowed down outside of a house with a sagging chain-link fence. He put the car in park, leaving the keys in the ignition and the motor running.

"I have to run outside and talk to this guy for a second." He opened his door and climbed out.

I didn't think anything of it. I rolled my window down. The sound of barking dogs filled the car. I waited for the scream of police sirens, expecting them at any moment.

Dad walked around to my side of the car and shook his head at me. "Roll the window up." His eyes shifted from side to side, keeping watch all around. "Keep the doors locked. I'll be right back."

I did as he said. With the windows up, the sounds from outside were muffled. I tried to keep an eye out in all directions. This was the man who put his child in the backseat with three convicts. What—or who—did Dad think was worse? Was someone going to try to steal the car? I watched him in my side mirror. Dad grabbed a bag out of the trunk. A light-skinned black man with short hair approached. Brand new Nikes were tied tightly around his feet, and a thick gold chain that looked like rope hung around his neck. He looked like he was in his mid-twenties. Dad shook his hand. They chatted for a moment, and then Dad followed him down the sidewalk. As soon as they disappeared around the corner, my heart really started to pound.

I fiddled with the radio buttons, aligned all the vents, anything I could do to keep my hands busy so I wouldn't notice them shaking. Every flickering movement in the corner of my vision made me jump. *Hurry up, Dad.* I was so busy trying to keep my cool that I didn't see someone walk up a few minutes later. The rap of knuckles against the driver's-side window startled me. I pushed myself up against the opposite door, ready to make a run for it.

"Hey, let me in," a voice said. A moment later Dad's face appeared in the window. He knocked again. "Devin, unlock the door."

I leaned across the seat and pulled the knob.

Dad smiled as he got in. He was in a good mood. I didn't say anything until we were well out of the neighborhood and my pulse had returned to a normal rate.

"What were you doing back there, Pops?"

He didn't look over at me. "Oh, you know. Everyone out here is hustling, trying to do their thing. I'm just trying to help these young kids."

I couldn't put my finger on it, but I knew something shady had gone down. By the time we got home, the whole scene barely registered on my emotional memory. It got lost in the rest of the chaos.

After a while I realized that my parents weren't just doing drugs; they were selling them, too. Dad bought enough for himself and Mom, plus some extra that he parceled out to a few street runners. Obviously he didn't know how to make the pyramid scheme work; he never saw much profit from this endeavor, but it was enough to help fund both his and Mom's habits.

I was hurt and disappointed when I found out, surprised even though I shouldn't have been. My parents were experts at gaming the system and avoiding their financial responsibilities. When Dad got in an accident with the Buick, his insurance paid for a weeklong rental from Enterprise while his car was in the shop. We drove that car around for three weeks. He didn't think anything of it until Enterprise threatened to call the police and report it stolen.

When the drug use came out from behind my parents' bedroom door to stare me right in the face, I kept my eyes focused straight ahead. Several years of St. John's had convinced me that the military was not for me, and my parents' lifestyle didn't appeal to me. At school, the underlying assumption was that we would all go to college. It was the clear option, but I didn't have any role models in my life that went through higher education. No one in my social circle and no one in my family had any experience with college.

The only people I could look to as examples were the varsity players who were on their way to play college basketball. Ron Steptoe, Grayson Marshall, Rodney Rice—I watched a plethora of guys from our team walk out onto college courts. I wanted to be like them. By the end of my first year on the JV team, I knew I wanted to play college ball. We didn't lose a single game that season. My grade point average hovered around 3.3; for not putting in too much work, that seemed reasonable. Basketball was my golden ticket. I never discussed it with my parents—it had been assumed for so long that I had internalized it.

That summer, the sports world was shocked by the untimely death of Len Bias. A high school legend from the DC area, Len became all-American as a forward at the University of Maryland. He was the second pick in the NBA draft, snapped up by the Boston Celtics as their number one choice. Two days later he died of cardiac arrhythmia from a cocaine overdose. He was only twenty-three years old. Len never got his shot at the pros. That cemented it; I was scared to death of drugs. Basketball had to get me into college.

CHAPTER 14

RECONNAISSANCE

AFTER CHASING HOOKERS FROM THE TENDER AGE OF TWELVE, the day-to-day routine of high school didn't hold my attention. There were times when I was totally present. When I felt challenged, I rose to the occasion; I could get the un-gettable girls, I could handle any crazy situation Dad threw at me. I excelled in isolated pockets of life, but I spent the majority of my teenage years either bored or daydreaming about having a better life. I needed spontaneity, variety. Even though I wanted stability, I craved opportunities to see something new.

Part of my quest to keep myself out of the house was to get a part-time job. I had run a newspaper route for a few years when I was a kid, but it didn't fulfill my need for variety. To pick up girls, I needed money and the opportunity to meet them. Early in my high school career I picked up a job at Jerry's Sub Shop. Jerry's sold pizza and steak-and-cheese sandwiches. New people came through the door every day; it was perfect for me.

At Jerry's, I met my first white girlfriend, Kelley Burns. She was pale, with brown hair and blue eyes— really cute. I was smitten right off the bat. We flirted for a month before I finally got the nerve to ask her out.

I pulled up to her house in Dad's Buick. It was in an exclusive neighborhood where the homes were huge. How was I going to fit in here? Maybe I should just leave. After a few minutes of indecision, I got out of the car.

Her mom greeted me at the door. "Hi! You must be Devin. Come on in."

Inside, a tall white man gave me an appraising look.

"Come right on in," her mom repeated. She ushered me through the entry toward the den.

A diploma from Cornell University proclaimed her family's high station. Once again, I connected the dots between that education and this lifestyle. Thankfully, Kelley bounded down the stairs and saved me from her father's cool disinterest.

"Oh, don't worry about Daddy," she said when I mentioned his aloof demeanor. "I brought a black guy home once—just as a friend to hang out with—and now he wants to check out any guy who wants to date me. He doesn't trust black people."

I took her downtown to look at the Washington monuments. We grabbed a blanket, something to eat, and a couple of sodas and sat there looking at the Jefferson Memorial or Abe Lincoln. We lingered there until the lights came on, illuminating the stone structures in the dark.

We dated on and off throughout the year. She never told her father I was biracial. Her mom knew, though; it was our little secret.

Working together at Jerry's was a lot of fun. Unfortunately, I was a terrible employee. I stood on the back line cracking jokes with one of the other guys while orders for pizzas piled up. White tickets hung in the window, but we ignored them.

"Hey, pass me one of those pans," I said to the guy with whom I was supposed to be cooking.

"What are you going to do with that?"

"I'm making myself a pizza." I grabbed the pan from his hands and started to assemble the fattest personal pan pizza I'd ever seen. I threw steak and peppers onto the crust and piled it high with cheese.

"Man, you are going to be in so much trouble," my coworker laughed.

"Why? You going to rat me out? I'm making you one, too."

We stood and watched the two pans roll through the machine. The smell of melting cheese and crisping crust made my stomach growl.

"I've been waiting on a large pepperoni for twenty minutes!" one of our other coworkers yelled from the front of the store.

"Yeah, we'll get to it!" I shouted back. A pepperoni pizza took almost no effort, but I was not interested in doing any work.

Our pizzas slowly came through the end of the machine. We dropped them on the counter and cut them into slices. Right as I took my first steaming bite the manager stormed into the kitchen.

"What's going on back here?" He took one look at me with the pizza in my mouth and his face turned dark. Without a word he threw together the ingredients for the pizza order we hadn't started yet. After the orders were under control he took me back to the office.

"Devin, it's just not working out having you here. I have to let you go."

I knew I was an atrocious worker, so I shouldn't have been surprised, but I was embarrassed that I got caught and fired for eating a pizza. The walk of shame out of the restaurant was humiliating.

Shortly after leaving Jerry's, I found a new job at an Amoco gas station. For six to eight hours at a time, I sat behind a Plexiglas window and took money from strangers in exchange for cigarettes and gasoline. That job suited my lack of work ethic a little better, but I knew the gas station wouldn't lead me to the bigger, better life I spent so much time daydreaming about.

Basketball and academics would be my ticket to a better life. I relied on that assumption to get me through my junior year at St. John's. At this point the turbulence at home had turned me into an emotional zombie. I did reasonably well in basketball, but even on the courts I wasn't a hard worker. Natural talent had gotten me this far, and I didn't put forth any extra effort; I took the easy route whenever possible.

Joe Gallagher coached St. John's varsity program. Everyone in the DC area knew Joe and his boys. I'd heard about him and his track record since seventh grade. Back in the day, playing for Coach Gallagher was this intangible dream I could barely imagine. By the time I stepped onto his court, I was so zoned out that I couldn't even appreciate the opportunity. We butted heads from the moment I made varsity.

I loved to compete and hang out with my friends, but I didn't have the drive to put in the extra work after mandatory practices. The dysfunction at home bled into every facet of my life. My parents came to as many games as they could, given their work schedules—Mom to every home game and Dad to almost all of them. Standing in the middle of the court waiting for tipoff, I'd look through the crowd of screaming fans and wonder if people could tell how burned out Mom looked. Every time Dad came to watch, I'd worry about someone bumping into him or saying the wrong thing and triggering another outburst.

The ball flew halfway down the court before I reacted; it disappeared in a sea of pounding sneakers and sweating limbs. All I could think was, *please let my parents be normal.* My worst games were against mediocre opponents. While I jogged down the hardwood I scanned the crowd for girls, the only thing that could hold my attention for more than a few minutes. The lack of motivation I displayed both on and off court got me benched for a good part of my junior year.

"What are you doing, Hughes?" Coach Gallagher yelled from the sidelines during practice. "I told you to play defense. Play defense!"

I hated defense. It required too much effort. I didn't want to be the fastest cat in the jungle; I just wanted to be a little faster than the slowest. The player I was supposed to be guarding went in for a layup and scored.

Gallagher blew the whistle. The rest of the team trotted toward the water fountains. I waited to face the coach.

"What are you doing out there?"

I shrugged. "Why do I have to practice if you're not going to play me?"

"I don't play you because you don't play hard all the time."

"Maybe I would if you put me in more often."

"Can you honestly tell me that you're giving your all?"

"Yes." That was a lie and I knew it.

He threw his hands in the air, disgusted. "If you believe that, I have nothing else to say to you. You want to play, you put in the work and show me."

I bristled at the challenge. As soon as we hit the court for another scrimmage, I stayed with my man. I respected Coach Gallagher, and I knew he was trying to push me, but I didn't have the same connection with him that I'd had with my other coaches. I needed the constant challenge in order to perform. I didn't have the fire within me to bring out my best at every opportunity. If I didn't feel challenged, I could walk off the court with eight points or less in a night. I knew I let the team down a few times, but I just didn't have the drive to bring my A-game if I didn't have a worthy opponent.

The academic year passed without much notice on my part; I was completely disengaged. When it ended, I knew I had to do something to redeem myself. If next year went anything like this one, I wouldn't play college ball. Some of the other guys on my team talked about a one-week camp called Five-Star. I approached Mom with the idea as soon as I heard about it.

She'd just gotten home from work at her first job and she had to turn around and leave soon. I knocked on her bedroom door, wondering what state of lucidity I'd find her in.

"What do you want?" she asked as she opened the door.

"There's a basketball camp this summer that some of the guys are going to."

She threw a few things into her purse and hustled back to the hallway. "How much does it cost, Devin?"

"It's three, maybe four hundred dollars." I rushed to explain the benefits before she object to the price tag. "It's a good camp. A lot of college coaches go and it'll get me some good exposure."

There was no pushback; I'd said the magic word. *College*.

This camp was similar to the ones I went to when I was younger, but the atmosphere on that campus felt different. This one was further away, just outside of Pittsburgh. The daily routine consisted of breakfast, followed by stretching and quick discussion of fundamentals. After that, it was drills and scrimmages all day every day. By four in the afternoon, we were beat. We headed back to the dorms to shower and hang out. Here, I cracked on guys who became big-time basketball players. Dennis Scott came from the number one–ranked Flint Hill in Oakton, Virginia. He later went on to play at Georgia Tech and twelve years of NBA. Rodney Monroe played at St. Maria Goretti in Hagerstown, Maryland. Later, he played for North Carolina State University, was drafted by the NBA, and landed on an overseas team. I wasn't as good as they were, but my silver tongue earned me a place in their circle.

There were so many coaches with clipboards at our practices that you never knew who was watching. The guys I was here with were all-American. During drills I poured my heart and soul onto the court. I had to step up the intensity because I didn't want to be embarrassed. One of those guys with the clipboards had to notice me, had to.

The high of camp wore off soon after I came home. The experience validated my desire to play college ball, but my focus hadn't improved. One day I sat in the living room with Dad. I wasn't scheduled to work that day, so I was looking for an excuse to get out of the house and do something. I looked over at Dad and my eyes fell on the tattoo on his right arm.

"Hey, Dad," I said. "Let's go get me a tattoo."

He sat up. "Yeah, sure. Let's do it."

Next thing I knew I was in the chair at a tattoo shop in DC, looking through books of sample art. There was no significance or symbolism to the whim. I flipped through the stock material until I saw something I recognized. Bo Brady on *Days of Our Lives* had a tattoo of a heart with a dagger through it. He looked pretty cool. I pointed to a similar design.

"That's the one I want."

As soon as I saw the lines on my skin I knew I didn't want it. *This is crazy. How am I going to sell myself to a good school with this?*

"What do you think?" the skinny girl who'd drawn it asked.

Dad peered at it. "Looks good to me."

I couldn't chicken out with Dad standing right there. I'd said I wanted it. Now I had to man up and follow through.

"Have a seat." The girl pointed at a padded leather chair. "Wrap your arms around the front and try not to move." She dipped her needle into the black ink and it started to buzz. "This might hurt a little."

When the tip of the needle burrowed into the back of my shoulder it hurt like hell. *I don't want this!* I screamed in my head. On the outside I stayed cool and strong. We didn't tell Mom.

"What is that?" Mom snapped the first time she saw my shoulder.

"Nothing."

"Don't lie to me, let me see that."

I reluctantly pulled my shirt to the side.

She leaned in and looked at it. "Division I schools don't want tattooed people running around their campuses."

She always knew exactly what to say to make it personal. I felt stupid for following through with the impulse.

My game didn't improve right away my senior year. I continued to play down to the level of competition I felt from the opposing team; occasionally I played up, but only when I thought the other players were exceptionally good. Under pressure, I played on fire. Thirty-point games weren't unusual for me when we faced notoriously tough teams. That was my modus operandi in everything I did. Even in academics I could have pushed harder, done better. My grade point average hovered around 3.4. If I tried, I could've hit 3.9 easily, but I didn't want to put in any more work than I absolutely had to. Coach Gallagher didn't start me right away that season. I sat on the sidelines and watched my team sprint back and forth without me.

How am I going to get to play college ball if I'm not even playing? The realization hit me out of the blue as I sat there, watching. If I wanted the results, I'd have to put in the effort. If and when I got onto the court, I wouldn't let Gallagher pull me off all season.

The coach put me in halfway through the first quarter. The team played well, and I scored eighteen points for a solid victory. I was on fire.

Coach Gallagher stopped me after the game. "I have been waiting for you to arrive for a year and a half." He shook my hand. "I look forward to having you around."

I started every other game that year.

After practice one day, Coach Gallagher called me into his office. He sat with his head down, peering at a stack of papers.

I knocked lightly on the door. "You wanted to see me?"

He looked up from his paperwork. Without a word, he pointed at a row of envelopes sitting at the edge of his desk. One of them had my name on it.

My heart beat time and a half. I'd heard about this from the upper class. I grabbed the envelope and ran outside. In the top-left corner, Nebraska's logo proclaimed my success in bold letters. Nebraska had a great football team. This was my hall pass to a better future. I tucked it into my bag and ran home to tell my parents.

Dad couldn't sit still as soon as I gave them the news. "I told you. I *told* you. You're meant for more."

"You just keep that ball rolling," Mom chimed in. "You have to keep hustling. This is your ticket to college."

I basked in the positive affirmation and excitement. My parents kept talking, but I didn't listen. I read that letter eight times before I let them take it from me. Both of them took it to work to show off. We never celebrated; we simply accepted it with pride.

"It's all coming together," Dad said, as if he'd planned this all along.

"Absolutely," I said to his face. Behind his back, I snickered. Anyone who thought my parents had this master plan worked out was on more drugs than they were. I let them maintain that illusion. I was the glue holding together two people with special needs.

Colgate, Nebraska, Rutgers, Temple, Cornell, Le Moyne. Just seeing those brochures and inquiries pile up on the dining room table felt like validation; I had a future. I was ecstatic. In my mind, I was headed for Division I. I didn't know that athletes got these letters all the time—that they were nothing more than a "Hey, good luck this season, we'll be watching." I didn't realize that getting inquiries wouldn't automatically translate into scholarship offers, so to me, college already seemed like a given.

I had been the responsible one for years already, but now my parents started treating me more like an adult. Dad sat me down repeatedly to address the substance issue.

"Look, if you want to start drinking, you need to do that here with us."

"Okay." I brushed the comment aside. The last thing I wanted was to end up like him and Mom for the rest of my life.

"I mean it. That goes for drugs, too." He looked me in the eye, more serious than I remembered seeing him in a long time. "There's a lot of bad stuff out there that can make you sick if you don't know what's in it. If you want to smoke dope, you do it here, where we know it's safe."

"Right, Dad."

He shrugged, and that was the end of the conversation. The usual upbeat persona shone through and he was back to cracking jokes. I didn't even know where to begin to try to make sense of his crazy logic. I had no desire to do drugs, least of all with my parents, but that was normal for them. They didn't think twice about it.

The letters of interest came in from several schools, but the coach from Colgate actually called our house.

Dad answered the phone. "Hello?" He broke out in a grin and waved me over. "Yes. Oh, really? That's great."

I gave him a quizzical look.

"Next week is fine. We look forward to meeting with you." He said good-bye and set the phone back in the receiver.

"Who was that?"

"That was the head coach of Colgate! He saw you at camp this summer and he wants to come here and meet with you next week to talk about you coming to play for him next year."

I couldn't believe it. Dad wrapped his arms around me in a bear hug; I stood there and let it happen. The news didn't sink in right away.

"I'm going to call your mother. We're going out to celebrate."

The mood of house changed completely after that phone call. Both of my parents were ecstatic. They strutted around and acted as though their long-established plans were finally coming together. They took me to our favorite buffet restaurant to commemorate that phone call.

Dad walked back and forth between our booth and that buffet several times. Every time he came back with a Mount Everest of food balanced on his plate. I eyed the giant mound on his second plate while I picked at my first.

Damn, dude, I thought. *You don't have to get it all in one trip; you* can *go back.* The stack of empty plates in front of us grew quickly. Normally I would have been embarrassed, but that night we were all so happy it didn't matter. All three of us saw the light at the end of the proverbial tunnel. I was going to college.

A week after the coach called, he arrived at the house. I spent the entire morning cleaning, but no amount of polish would make our secondhand lifestyle new and shiny. My parents both took time off work to be there at 4:30 to meet him. Dad dressed up like he was going to church. Mom put on new makeup and even did her hair; they were both dressed to impress. Both were clear-eyed and lucid. They sat in the living room and waited while I scoured the place, looking for the bongs and pipes I was sure I missed.

"Go put on your khakis and a nice shirt," Mom told me half an hour before the coach was scheduled to arrive.

I ran up the stairs to my room. Like the coach would care how I was dressed if he found a bong between the sofa cushions. I pulled on clean clothes and went back downstairs to wait with them. We sat there in silence. Would the coach see through our biracial Brady Bunch act? I couldn't sit still. Had I found all of Mom's baggies?

I ran to the door when he knocked. Mom and Dad slowly got to their feet behind me.

"Hi, I'm Joe Baker," the coach said and shook my hand. He wore slacks and a short-sleeved shirt. His smile didn't quite reach his eyes.

I didn't hear anything else he said; I was too worried about what he would think about our raggedy house. *Please don't let Dad say anything stupid.*

My parents felt comfortable with him because he was black.

"I'm Clarkie Hughes, and this is my wife, Gloria," Dad said, pumping the coach's hand up and down enthusiastically. "Come on in, Coach." He led the way to the living room.

"This is my first year at Colgate, and I'm excited to put my stamp on the program," he said with another smile. "I think it would be a great fit for Devin."

Mom beamed. Dad hung on every word. Couldn't they see he was a salesman? He didn't act black; he seemed like an Uncle Tom to me. I stared at the floor, willing my father into silence.

"Devin's a shooter," Coach Baker continued. He leaned back against the couch. The vinyl cover crackled beneath his shifting weight.

"That's my boy," Dad said.

"He can put the ball up and get it in the basket. He'll be a good asset to the team."

"How does the rest of the team look?" Dad asked.

I closed my eyes. Why was he asking questions? He didn't know what he was talking about. This was the longest I'd ever heard him go without torpedoing the conversation with the F-bomb.

"We have another player from the St. John's program already on the team," he said.

Dave Crittenden was on the varsity team at St. John's when I started JV. I was a little annoyed that he would compare me to Dave, but I didn't have time to dwell on it. Any moment my parents were going to do something stupid and I was going to have to hustle Coach Baker out the door.

"Coach Gallagher runs a good program. I'm sure Devin will do well playing at Colgate."

He sat in our living room for an hour. Every minute was a silent agony as I prayed to any god who would listen to please get this man out of my house. The more comfortable my parents felt, the more likely they were to say something crazy and blow my chances.

"You could stay for dinner," I heard Mom offer.

My stomach twisted itself into a knot. *Please don't accept, please don't accept.*

"I appreciate the offer, ma'am, but I've got another appointment to make."

Salvation was at hand. I shook hands with him again as he left.

"I'm excited to have you come check out the university in the spring."

I nodded. I couldn't speak. Relief turned my knees to jelly as I watched him walk away. My parents had made it through the entire interview without saying anything embarrassing. I couldn't do much about the shabby state of the house, but at least the coach wouldn't associate me with a couple of crazy drug addicts.

As soon as the door shut, my parents started talking at me. They were hooked.

Mom smiled. "That was the head coach of Colgate, Devin."

"He is going to take care of you," Dad said.

"Yeah, we'll see." Colgate was Division I. I wasn't ready to put blind trust into everything the coach said on a recruiting trip, but I was excited.

Blind faith led me to assume that because I played basketball at St. John's, I would get into a good college. I would've gone without basketball, but I was ill pre-pared. My parents didn't know anything about how to apply. No one asked about majors, minors, professors, or life after college. I never did any work to prepare: no campus visits, no letters to admissions offices. I let the game lead me.

CHAPTER 15

CRUMBLING WALLS

A FEW MONTHS INTO SENIOR YEAR, MY COOL, COLLECTED FAÇADE CRACKED. The visit from Coach Baker revved me up for the prospect of college, but every minute I spent under my parents' roof negated that drive. I was restless. I loved my parents, but knowing I was headed for college made it harder to live in their house with the drugs and dysfunction. My emotional void consumed everything in its path, and I continued to be inconsistent in both academics and athletics.

One night, in the middle of the fourth quarter, I caught the eye of a slim brunette I hadn't seen around any of my regular hangouts before. We were up by twelve points. The pace of the game lagged; our opponents had accepted defeat. I'd stopped trying five minutes into the third quarter. I jogged back and forth across the court; I let the ball lead me without trying to interfere with its path.

The ball reversed direction, and the floorboards bounced as both teams charged toward our opponents' basket. I hesitated. The girl smiled at me. Her teeth shone against the gleam of red lipstick. I gave her a quick nod and jogged after my team, my brain on autopilot. By the time I reached the top of the key, we'd stolen the ball and I had to turn around and run back.

I was far ahead of the pack. The ball flew toward me. It snapped against my palms and I jumped up for the layup. It whooshed through the net. I looked back at the girl. She smiled. For the remainder of the quarter, if I make a basket or a good play I looked over at her. Amidst the chaos of the crowd, I felt as if we were the only two people in the gym, sharing a slow dance at center court that I knew would be over as soon as the whistle blew.

We won, despite my lack of personal investment in the second half. I changed as slowly as possible. An unexplainable sense of dread grew inside my chest every time I thought about going home. I needed a time-out. Denial and rationalization could only go so far. So many thoughts collided in my head at once that I couldn't pick out a single one other than *I can't go back there*. I didn't fully understand why. Nothing had significantly *changed*; I just felt exhausted at the idea of returning to the mess of our townhouse. The rest of the team celebrated around me, but I barely heard the din.

I walked out of the locker room twenty minutes later, the keys to Dad's Riviera biting into my palm. A few lingering fans stood in small clusters on the court. Somewhere outside the gym, I knew Mom and Dad waited for me. It was already nine o'clock. Mom had to be at work in an hour, but Dad would be at home all night. My chest tightened as I walked toward the double doors. *I can't go back there. Not tonight.*

"Hey." A girl's voice broke into the noise in my head— it was the cute brunette from the bleachers. Her blue eyes crinkled with a friendly smile. I immediately looked at her hands. Her skin was smooth and white, her fingernails clean. The incessant voice in my head quieted.

"Yeah? Did you enjoy the game?"

"It was good. You played pretty well."

I looked around the gym to keep from staring at her red lipstick. "Are you here by yourself?"

"No. My sister is a friend of one of the guys you beat

tonight." She waved at a small cluster of people. "That's her right there." The girl who waved back looked just like her. "So what are you doing tonight?" she asked. "I'd love to get to know you."

"Nothing." I started walking toward the doors. I knew she'd follow. "I have to go say bye to my parents real quick." We walked out of the gym and I scanned the loitering crowd for Mom and Dad. I shivered. The air was just cool enough that a jacket would have been nice. The *I-can't-go-back* mantra crept into my thoughts. Dad waved as soon as he saw me. "Wait here," I told her. "I'll be right back."

"Good game tonight," Dad called out. He put one arm around my shoulders. Mom didn't say anything.

I slipped out from under Dad's arm. "I'm going to go grab a bite to eat with this girl." I didn't even know her name yet.

They followed the nod I threw back over my shoulder. Mom turned to Dad. "I'll drop you off on the way to work so Devin can take your car."

"Okay, but don't stay out too late," Dad said with a wink.

"I'll take her home right afterwards." Even as I said it, the words felt like a lie. *I can't go home.* The horrible feeling in my chest eased as I said good-bye to them and turned back to the girl.

"I'm all yours," I told her. "What's your name, by the way?"

She grinned. "I'm Amy. Can we give my sister a ride home first?"

"Anything you want." We waited for her sister to break away from the crowd and then walked to the parking lot. I pointed out the beige Riviera. Amy rode shotgun and her sister slid into the backseat. "Where do you live?"

We didn't talk on the way to their house, except when she gave me directions. As we drove into southeast DC, the neighborhood got progressively more run down. What were these two lily-white girls doing living over here? Could she be setting me up? I kept an eye on all three mirrors; this was not a neighborhood you wanted anyone to surprise you in. My mind conjured images of Aunt Fanny's bullet-riddled walls. Dad's warning not to trust anybody dueled with my desire not to go home. By the time we pulled up outside their house—one of many like it on a row of low brick buildings—I'd worked myself into full-blown paranoia.

"Do you want to come in?" she asked, her hand on the door handle. Her sister slammed the back door shut. She ran up the white porch stairs.

I looked at the beaters parked on either side of the street. Dad's car was nicer than anything in a two-block radius. The light over the porch was dim; it barely lit the sagging steps. I shook my head. "No, thanks. I'll wait here." As soon as she got out, I reached back and pushed down the knob to lock the door behind me. The red leather seat squeaked as I slouched down as far as I could. I left the car in gear, my foot pressed hard against the brake. This was one stakeout I didn't have to sit through if I didn't want to; the first sign of anything sketchy, I was out of there.

A few minutes and no ambushes later, Amy came out of the house wearing a heavier jacket.

"Where to?" I didn't care where we went, so long as it wasn't this neighborhood.

"Take a left two blocks up. There's an all-night coffee shop that serves breakfast all day not too far from here."

The restaurant was a stereotypical diner. The place was surprisingly busy for a late night. Red vinyl booths butted up against plate-glass windows, and the air smelled like old grounds and fryer grease. A crowd of bar-goers laughed at a table near the door. We sat across each other at a booth near the back and ordered food. I got bacon and eggs, and Amy ordered chocolate chip pancakes.

"So you like basketball?" I asked.

"I play varsity at my school." She leaned forward as we talked, her hair cascading over her shoulders and toward the table.

This was the first time a girl had initiated the connection, approaching *me*, and I was intrigued. I leaned toward her. Our heads were mere inches from each other.

"Really?" I asked. "What school do you go to?"

She told me the name of a private girls' school I hadn't heard of. I played with the paper wrapper from my straw. "That's cool. What do your parents do?"

Asking the girl questions was normal for me. At home I never asked questions; in most cases I didn't want to hear the answers. I buried my questions, bottled them up, dragged them down into the cellar of my mind. Here it was safe. This little coffee shop was far enough away from home, literally and emotionally, that she could say anything. I could ride whatever wave came along tonight.

"My dad works for the government." She looked me right in the eyes and pushed a lock of hair behind her ear.

I couldn't help but smile back. This wasn't how I usually chased girls. It felt strange not to be the hunter, but it was pleasant. She was new, different, and I was so relieved to be anywhere other than home that I would've enjoyed myself even without the bizarre connection I felt to this girl I hardly knew.

Our food arrived half an hour into our discussion. We talked about a lot of superficial subjects: school, basketball, getting ready for college. As our meal wound down, I panicked. This would come to an end and I would have to go home. *I can't go back. I don't want to.* The more we talked, the more I felt the urge to tell her something real.

I waited for a natural break in the conversation. "You probably think I'm white, don't you?"

Amy cocked her head to one side and gave me a strange look. "Why do you say that?"

"I'm just curious. Do you?"

She leaned back in her seat, distancing herself a little from the topic. "Yeah, I guess so."

I pushed forward. "I get that a lot. There's more to me than what you see. I'm actually mixed."

"Really? Is your mom or your dad …"

"My dad's black." I filled in the blanks for her.

The rest of the conversation was like Ponce de Leon with a Christopher Columbus twist. I was curious why such a snow-white girl was living in southeast DC, and I never had the biracial conversation with white people.

We asked each other questions, the answers leading us to unexpected places. From my limited exposure to my Caucasian heritage, I was always worried that racism was a latent genetic trait buried inside every white person's DNA. With this girl, that didn't seem to be an issue.

"So what's it like, being both?" she asked, genuinely interested.

"It's like being torn between two different worlds. People everywhere preach that race isn't important, but it's everywhere."

"That's so true." She leaned her elbows on the table and gesticulated with her hands as she talked. "And it's not just white and black. I hear white people putting down Mexicans or laughing at Polish kids all the time."

"And in the black world, there are divisions between the dark and light skinned. My dad got it all the time when he was younger, from his own family. As much as people like to say we live in a colorblind society, everybody needs to associate themselves with a tribe."

"Some commonality."

"And race is always the most obvious one." I was exhilarated, on fire. This was my own little experiment, my private exploration into what it could be like, owning both parts of me out loud.

"You look white. So does that mean you …" She seemed to be searching for a particular word. After a moment she threw up her hand in surrender. "Do you … *feel* white?"

The moment of truth. I took a deep breath and considered the answer. Every time I identified myself as black, I felt as if I were going through security at the airport and declaring myself a citizen of an enemy country. But I had never identified as white. I thought of the day I'd taken my SATs, when I'd had to check a box for my race. I stared at the form for so long my vision started to blur. I could have checked White if I had wanted to. I should have checked Asian, just to see if anyone read those things. In the end, I scrawled a hurried dash by Other and submitted my paperwork.

"No," I said now to Amy. "I don't feel white. I've grown up with a black experience. It's a weird feeling."

"What do you mean?"

"Well, let's say I looked black, with the facial features and the hair. Then it'd be obvious to everybody that my gene pool is mixed, and people would expect me to act black. I don't look black, but I grew up with all black people, so I act black. It's like I'm going through an entire basketball game wearing the opposing team's jersey. With Mom being white and Dad being black, it's a constant reminder that I just don't fit."

These were thoughts I never expressed at home, but in this conversation, with this girl, it felt cathartic to articulate the ideas and pressures I couldn't escape anywhere else. I sat there and disassembled the wall between my two halves brick by brick. In that diner, I finally found a way to put into words the reasons I didn't want to go home.

After leaving the restaurant, we drove around until we found a place to park. We fooled around a little bit, but mostly we just talked. Time flew by and the confession still poured out of me. I didn't get into my parents' drug use—that I never shared with anyone—but I unpacked every piece of baggage I carried around regarding coming to terms with my identity. Amy was a life raft in the midst of a vast ocean of insecurity waiting for me at home, and I clung to our conversation as long as I could.

The streets were quiet when I finally drove her home. Street lamps cast small pools of weak light against the darkness as we wound our way through blocks of unkempt residential properties. We had both run out of things to say. The spark of our brief, intense emotional connection flickered. Without one of us to blow oxygen on it, it would die. We both knew it. I could almost feel it dying right there. I savored the little moment that we had; I knew there probably wouldn't be another because that new-car smell would wear off and our next encounter wouldn't be as real, as raw, as our initial attraction.

Outside her house she leaned over to kiss me goodnight. Her lips were soft as they pressed against mine. I put my hand against her cheek, then let my fingers run through her beautiful brown hair. When she broke away, she scribbled something on a slip of paper. She looked me in the eye and curled my fingers around the paper. Her phone number was scrawled across it in loopy blue Bic. I didn't give her mine. I watched her walk into the house, and that was the last I saw of her.

I didn't know exactly how late it was, but I knew I'd be in trouble if I showed up at home now. Mom's work wasn't too far away. I headed for the hospital before I even had my story straight.

Mom worked at one of the reception desks near the front doors. I shuffled slowly across the floor, playing up a fake affliction. As soon as she saw me, Mom hauled herself out of her chair and rushed toward me.

"Boy, where have you been? It is three thirty in the morning. We've been freaking out. Your dad is calling every five minutes wondering where you are."

"Mom?" I peered at her as though I didn't recognize her, then launched into my lie. "Mom, I went out to dinner with this girl and we were just hanging out and I started to feel woozy."

The anger visibly melted from her face, morphing into concern. She put her palm against my forehead.

"Next thing I knew I woke up in the car by myself and I don't even know how I got here."

She patted down my arms and legs. "Well, you're not bleeding. Does anything hurt?"

"No, Mom, I'm fine."

"What happened?"

I pulled a lie out of the air. "I left the table to go to the bathroom during dinner and I think she put something in my drink."

"Did she take your wallet?"

"No."

"Did she do anything to the car?"

"No, Mom, it's fine."

She folded me into a hug and patted me down again. I had to bite my lip to keep from laughing out loud.

"We'll get you checked out just in case. Come here."

Mom dragged me over to the nurses' station. "This is my son. He said a girl put something in his drink.

Can you have someone check him out while I go call his father?"

A small swarm of medical people buzzed around me. They shone a penlight in my eyes, took my pulse, and asked a bunch of ridiculous questions. They all bought it.

"Doesn't look like he's suffering any lingering side effects," one of the nurses told Mom when she hung up with Dad. "He'll probably be fine, but you might want to keep an eye on him for a little while."

"Okay, thank you." Mom led me to a chair in the waiting room where she could see me from her desk. I played my part. It was late, so acting tired wasn't hard. Mom brought me a soda and came to check on me every few minutes for an hour. By four thirty, I was more bored than anything else.

"I'm sorry," I said when Mom came back the next time. "I shouldn't have gone out with someone I didn't know."

Mom waved her hand dismissively. "Are you okay to drive home?"

"Yeah, I think so."

Just as I expected, that was the end of it. Mom had moved on. I drove home, shocked at how easy it had been. Dad was less forgiving. He was waiting for me in the living room when I finally arrived half an hour later.

"Boy, what did I tell you about trusting people?" His eyes blazed with anger.

I shrugged. Playing the victim card wasn't going to work—Mom had already told him I was fine.

"So this girl put something in your drink? Were you

drinking alcohol? I told you if you want to drink, you're going to do it here with us."

I was exhausted. I didn't want to own up to the fact that I just didn't want to come home; I just wanted to go to bed. "No, I didn't have any alcohol."

"You are going to get yourself in a sling, running around with girls you don't know."

"Yeah, Dad, I know. Look, I'm tired. I'm just going to sleep it off, all right?"

Dad gave me another long look. "You should have called."

I wondered what he would say, knowing that—for the first time—I had trusted someone with my least understood possession: my identity.

CHAPTER 16

BRANCHING OUT

BETWEEN THE ONE DATE I SHARED WITH AMY AND

EARLY SPRING, I went through several fits and starts of cabin fever, though I never felt the same panic I had that night. Basketball season was winding down. Our team played to sold-out crowds every night. Toward the end of the season, we lost a game against our archrival, DeMatha, and ended up in the consolation against McKinley Tech High School. The game took place at Cole Field House on the campus of the University of Maryland. Shortly thereafter we had the opportunity to play in the Alhambra Catholic Invitational Tournament, where we made it to the finals and lost to DeMatha again in the championship. That was my final high school game, and we ended the year with twenty-nine wins and five losses.

As the madness of the regular season came to a close, the phones of St. John's players started to jingle with calls from recruiters. Erik Harris and Eddie Reddick were headed to the Naval Academy, Scott Lamond to Gettysburg College, and Robert Harris to Shenandoah University to play hoops.

Coach Baker, of course, had invited me to visit Colgate, and I also had an invitation to go see another New York school, Le Moyne College in Syracuse. My mom handled the scheduling with both universities and set up visits for me on consecutive weekends in March. The first visit would be Colgate, which, in the upstate city of Hamilton, was an hour's drive after the hour-long flight.

My parents strutted through the DC airport with me. Dad made sure the check-in agent knew I was on my way to interview with a Division I school. I kept my mouth shut and hoped they wouldn't do anything too embarrassing before I could leave them behind for the weekend.

The plane was a small regional jet, two rows of three seats on either side of a narrow aisle. I sat in a window seat and watched the baggage handlers scurry underneath the wings. Back at the terminal I could see people waving from the giant windows, but I couldn't tell if any of them were my parents. For the first time since before the bonfire incident, I almost felt free.

In my mind, Colgate was the way to go. I'd be crazy to turn them down. The flight attendants started the safety briefings. I watched a blonde woman pantomime pulling an oxygen mask over her head without really hearing any of the instructions. When we landed in Syracuse an hour later, Coach Baker met me at the arrival gate. His Colgate windbreaker and cap were like the blinking lights of a landing strip, showing me the way. He smiled when he recognized me.

"Good to see you again, Devin."

I shook his hand. "Same here, Coach."

He gestured to a short black woman standing next to him. "This is Mrs. Baker, my wife."

"Nice to meet you, ma'am," I said, but I was taken aback. Why would he bring his wife to meet his new players? Was this standard recruiting procedure?

"Do you have any bags?" he asked.

"Just this one," I said, lifting the backpack I'd carried on.

"Excellent. Let's get a move on, then. We've got a

full schedule for you."

We walked out to the parking garage. I followed them to their car, not quite believing I was really here.

"How was your flight?" Mrs. Baker asked.

"It was fine, thank you."

The drive from Syracuse to Hamilton passed quickly. The coach and his wife kept up a steady stream of conversation along the way. Outside the car I watched the hustle and bustle of the big city dwindle into quiet, peaceful countryside. Every time we approached a larger town my heart beat faster. After an hour of false alarms, I forced myself to sit back in my seat and relax. I didn't even notice when we finally pulled into Hamilton.

"We're glad to have you here this weekend," Coach Baker said as the car slowed.

I snapped to attention. I felt like a kid with his nose pressed to a bakery window. The Colgate campus was gorgeous. Large stone buildings clustered around the quad, and despite the cold, stately green trees lined the sidewalks. Late afternoon sunlight filtered through the branches, giving the place an ethereal glow. It looked just like the brochures.

"We're going to have you stay with a couple of the guys on the team," the coach was saying as I gawked. "They'll give you a tour of the campus, and tomorrow I'll take you to see the gym. All you have to do is soak up as much of the experience as you can between now and Sunday morning."

Coach and Mrs. Baker handed me over to Jim Biegalski and Tony Horne, two sophomore-year players from the team. Jim was white, Tony black, and they shared an off-campus apartment with a Colgate football player. The first item on our itinerary was to swing by their place to drop off my bag. We strolled past the football field toward a two-story complex labeled College Street Apartments.

Their unit was right on the corner. As soon as we walked in I looked at everything with a critical eye. The carpet was low-grade, but clean enough. The furniture looked sturdy, with wooden arms and stain-resistant fabric on all the cushions. A couple of guys sat on the couch playing video games, all of them cracking on each other. Even though most of them were white, the setting felt natural to me.

Jim and Tony made me feel comfortable right from the start. They showed me the rest of the apartment, with its tiny kitchen and bathroom on the second floor. They fielded all the questions I dared to ask. I inquired about the current team, whether they liked the campus, and what the women were like. Then I asked what they thought of Coach Baker.

"He's a clown," Jim said without hesitation. "He doesn't know how to coach a winning team."

Tony agreed, then added, "Go put your stuff down and we'll take you on a quick tour."

Infatuation set in to stay. Colgate had this strange, wholesome feel—it was completely alien and somehow comforting at the same time. Coach Baker had pulled me out of the inner city and dropped me into the middle of Mayberry, and I loved it. Like DC, there were people everywhere, but here the constant hustle felt different. The campus population was an abundance of vanilla ice cream with a few chocolate sprinkles. Unlike home, this didn't cause me any concern. Instead of feeling uncomfortable like when Dad took me to predominantly white churches, here I felt like I could see how the other half lived.

The rest of the night passed in a whirl. I hung out with Jim and Tony and their friends. We ordered pizza and spent the night laughing and having a great time. As Friday ended, I couldn't believe how fast everything had gone. Twelve hours after saying good-bye to my parents I already knew I didn't want to go back.

Saturday morning I met with Coach Baker. He showed me the gym and took me to his office in the Reid Athletic Center. Framed credentials and photos of him and his past players covered one avocado-colored wall. Basketballs rolled around on the floor. A small metal fan sat in the windowsill, its motionless blades lying in wait for summer's heat. He sat down at his desk and laid his cards on the table.

"Look, Devin, I'm not going to pretend we're a great team. Not yet."

I nodded, finding myself drawn to his straightforward style. "I'm sure it's not easy to come in as a new coach and win right away."

"That's exactly right. As a team, we're not doing well at all. But we've got some great individual players and I've got big plans for next season. Big plans."

I didn't hear any of the negative; my brain interpreted the team's poor record as a chance for me to get more playing time as a freshman.

"We're a young team. There is nowhere for us to go but up."

After our short conversation he took me on another short tour and pointed out some of the university's administrative buildings. I barely heard him. I'd discovered yet another benefit to college life: college women. St. John's was an all-boys school. I still managed to find girls to chase just about everywhere, but here they roamed around in their natural habitat, all of them respectable—the kind I could take home to meet my mother, in the unlikely case I ever decided to take home one I liked. Awestruck, I stood rooted to the ground and marveled at the sheer number of them. *This is awesome.* The coach was black, so I felt comfortable joining the team even in a sea of mostly white faces; I wouldn't have to wear a uniform to class; there were ladies everywhere; and I was free from the drama and the drugs at home.

That night Jim and Tony introduced me to a couple of guys from Kappa Delta Rho. I'd heard about fraternities before and seen them on TV, but this was the first time I'd ever set eyes on one. On the approach from the street, I felt those Greek letters looming over me from above the porch. *This is so cool.* As soon as we walked through the front door I saw the chaos I expected to see in a frat.

Guys chased each other from one end of the house to the other, yelling words that ran together in an unintelligible cacophony. Every room of the house was filled to bursting with people. Couches crowded the living rooms. Some guys drank beer, some guys ate takeout, and all of them talked crap about each other. This felt like basketball camp. There weren't any frat parties that night, so we went out in a big group. The night passed in a blur. I couldn't get enough.

I met with Coach Baker again Sunday morning before we left. We faced each other over his desk in the athletic department. I sat in the same chair I had the day before.

Coach Baker sat on the edge of his chair, his elbows resting on the desk. "I hope you've been enjoying your visit so far," he said.

"You bet, Coach."

"We're excited about you coming here and playing for us in the fall."

"Yes, sir."

He picked up a pencil and balanced it on its eraser. "So where's your head at, Devin?"

"I love it. I love everything that's going on here, and I love what you're trying to do with the program."

The coach let out a small sigh; it might have been no more than a slightly deeper than normal breath. He drummed the pencil against the desktop. He seemed to be fishing for a particular answer, but I didn't know what he wanted.

"I'm just going to come right out and ask you. Can you see yourself here at Colgate?"

I grinned. "Absolutely. This is where I want to be. I will be here in the fall."

Coach Baker visibly relaxed. He settled back in his chair, the spring in the base creaking. "Well alright then," he said with a smile. The conversation flowed more freely between us. We talked about Dave Crittenden and how he was adjusting to college ball after leaving St. John's. I kept talking, but I didn't retain much of the information. I knew I would be coming to Colgate in the fall. I had a guaranteed way out of the toxic environment in my parents' townhouse. The future I had glimpsed at my math tutor's house had never seemed so tangible as it did in that moment.

When I landed back in DC on Sunday afternoon, I could hardly contain my excitement. I kept a poker face all the way home from the airport. Dad cooked a soul food dinner—black-eyed peas, collard greens, corn bread, and pork. We spent a rare evening around the dining room table, all three of us.

"So what did you think of the school?" Mom finally asked when we all sat down.

I couldn't keep the grin off my face anymore. "It was awesome. I loved it."

"Who did you meet?" Dad asked.

"I stayed with a couple of the guys from the basketball team."

"What did the campus look like?"

"It's nice. Lots of trees and old buildings. I told Coach Baker I want to play there in the fall."

"But you haven't even seen Le Moyne yet," Mom pointed out. She shoveled a forkful of beans into her mouth.

The swell in my chest deflated a little. Couldn't she see how perfect Colgate was? My mind was already made up. "Mom, Coach Baker said they wanted me."

"He expects you to look at other schools before

making up your mind."

"But I already gave him a verbal commitment." I looked to Dad for help, but he was in the middle of piling more food on his plate.

"Words don't mean anything," she said. "They've called twice in the last two weeks to confirm that you're coming next weekend."

"But—"

Mom gave me a look that said the time for debate was over.

"The Le Moyne coach seems like a good guy," Dad finally added.

I shrugged. Colgate was Division I. So the team wasn't great, but maybe I would get to play as a freshman. Best of all, it was a minimum of seven hours away from home, even with the flight. Le Moyne was Division II. There was nothing to decide. I didn't tell my parents any of that.

The following weekend I accepted the free trip and flew to Syracuse again. I wasn't in the same emotional state I had been in when I landed there seven days ago. This trip didn't feel as new or exciting. After arrival I scanned the crowd at the airport for Le Moyne's colors. The coach held a simple white sign with my name on it. He was white, and this was the first time I'd met him. I smiled at him and shook his hand, but my heart wasn't in it.

The coach tried to keep up the conversation, but I only half listened. As we drove through campus I couldn't help but compare everything to Colgate. The campus was small, quiet. The buildings looked older on the outside, at least in comparison to the idyllic image I remembered from the prior weekend.

I stayed in one of the dorms with one of the basketball players. He was nice, and I went through the motions, but there was nothing the guy could do or say at that point that would change my mind. All weekend I smiled and nodded, all the while daydreaming about wearing the Colgate uniform.

At home, Mom was satisfied that I at least checked out another school. She was the one who was on the phone with Coach Baker and the admissions office over the course of the next few weeks, getting all of my paperwork in line. I didn't do a thing but fill out the formal application when it arrived in the mail. The approval process wasn't a nerve-wracking experience for me as it was for normal high school seniors; I already knew I was in.

Still, the day I came home and found the big white envelope in the mail, I tore into it like a chocolate bar containing an elusive golden ticket.

"Mom!" I shouted as I ran into the house. It was a Saturday afternoon and she didn't have to be at work for hours yet. "Hey Mom, come look at this!" The paper shook in my hand.

Mom made her way down the stairs slowly. She was tired, half asleep. "What is going on? Why are you shouting?"

"Look!" I held the paper up in front of her face.

She squinted at the type. "Dear Devin, I am pleased to—"

"I'm in!" I interrupted her. She crushed me in a hug.

I savored the moment. With only a couple of months until graduation, and only a few more between that and the start of my new life, I was excited. My parents were excited, too; the plan they claimed to have had all along was finally coming together.

Once I knew there was a plan in place, I went on total autopilot. To me, the high school chapter of the book of my life was already over; it was time to move forward. Anything that didn't propel me closer to Colgate was a waste of time. Graduation was anticlimactic. The ceremony took place on the campus of Catholic University at the Basilica of the National Shrine of the Immaculate Conception in northeast DC. I didn't want to go, but both my parents took time off work. We had to wear our uniforms, so I looked like everybody else, just another face in the crowd.

I sat through the pomp and circumstance, rolling my eyes at my buddies and wishing the speeches were shorter. *Just hand out the diplomas already and let's get out of here.* In addition to being bored by the formal procedure, half of my brainpower was devoted to worrying about my parents. Every time they were together in a social setting I was paranoid that one of them would go off the deep end. I'd left the house early that morning, so I had no idea whether my mom had bothered to wash her hair. What if Dad hadn't taken his medication? Were they high?

After the ceremony we had dinner at the house. We didn't go out to celebrate. My parents both kept trying to make a big deal out of me graduating high school, but I couldn't muster the same enthusiasm. I already had both feet in the future.

One of the requirements for Colgate was that I get a physical. I went to the same pediatrician's office I'd been going to for years. Mom knew all the doctors and nurses here. I sat on the edge of the exam table as I waited for the doctor. A fit, Irish-looking woman about Mom's age came in with a clipboard. A nametag pinned to her chest proclaimed her as Sandy.

"And how are you today?" Sandy asked as she scanned my information. The top button of her blouse was undone; from my perch on the table, I could see right down her shirt.

The paper underneath me crackled as I shifted my weight. "I'm fine."

"I see you're getting your college physical."

"Yeah. I just graduated."

"And it's your birthday coming up, too." She gave me a coy smile over the top of the clipboard. "What are you going to do for your birthday?"

Is she flirting with me? I started talking about my plans for the summer, and how I was going to play for Colgate in the fall.

"So, Devin," she said, putting a hand on my knee. "What do you want for your birthday?"

She was definitely flirting. I went for it. "Sandy, you know what I want."

Sandy gazed at me, smiling. "You have to swear you're not going to talk to your mom about it."

Holy shit! I'd thrown a line in the water and landed a keeper! "Come on, of course I'm not going to tell my mom."

"Good. If she ever asks, I'll deny it." She scribbled something on a piece of paper and handed it to me. "Call me sometime and you can come over to my place."

I called her a few days later. She gave me directions to her apartment building. On the drive over, I still couldn't believe this was happening. When she opened the door in a bathrobe, I lost all my doubts.

We saw each other on and off throughout the summer. This wasn't a dating relationship; we never went out for dinner or to the movies, or to see the monuments. I showed up at her door, she answered wearing that bathrobe, and we made it happen. After we fooled around, there was always a sense of awkwardness in the air as I got up and left. I never told my friends or my parents. On the drive home, I wondered whether this was normal.

That summer, I also met my mom's friend Colleen at her office. She was flirty and funny and resembled Sandy physically. She was a lot more outgoing and gregarious where Sandy was serious and demure. With these older women, there was no expectation of the relationship turning into something more. I had conversations with these women that weren't normal teenage conversations; we talked about politics, religion, and current events. Between visits, I read the *Washington Post* to find topics to contribute.

I knew the relationships were finite. It was very much in the moment—enjoy it, have it, and let it go. I never told anyone about either Colleen or Sandy. A few times, I found myself in the same room as Colleen and my mom. That was surreal. The quiet smile on her face begged me not to tell my mother. I never did.

In the few months before orientation, I bounced between spending time with women and hanging out with my friends. We stayed out late, partying and having a blast. There was no drinking—we were all athletes—but a big group of us went to Ocean City in June for a beach blowout. A bunch of guys from the basketball team split the rent on a condo for five days.

The rest of the guys were black, and the area we stayed in was mostly white. We got strange looks everywhere we went, me in the middle of a pack of brothers. Their reactions didn't bother me; by now I was used to it, and there was a certain strength in numbers. We had a blast, picking up girls and joking and laughing with one another. Afterward, we all went our separate ways. It was the perfect end to our high school careers.

I couldn't wait to hit Colgate. I yearned for more than I had in my life. I wanted less chaos, I wanted good relationships, I wanted to stop being so guarded. In simple terms, I wanted to be normal. Although Dad had exposed me to a lot of situations other high schoolers wouldn't even dream about, in some ways I felt as if I'd been sheltered all my life. I had no idea how the other side of this race game worked. What might it be like to have white friends? To me, white was synonymous with normal. On TV, the traditional family units and nuclear families where all white. *Sanford and Son* was dysfunctional, *Good Times* was in the ghetto. *The Jeffersons* was an anomaly; I didn't know any black people who had moved on up. Celebrity athletes had made it, but I couldn't relate to them even through the lens of my black perspective; my friends always made fun of black celebrity athletes as white wannabes. It was the eighties. Jesse Jackson ran around preaching double standards. Everywhere I went, the message seemed to be that black people weren't getting their share. We had to fight, scratch, and claw our way out of our collective hole. I internalized all of that, packed it up with the rest of my baggage, and took it with me to college.

CHAPTER 17

PATTERN RECOGNITION

AFTER I GOT BACK FROM OCEAN CITY, MOM AND I CROSSED PATHS FOR THE FIRST TIME IN WEEKS.

She was on her way in from Friday's late shift while I was on my way out for the day.

"Hey, Mom," I said, reaching for the door handle. I didn't expect more than a grunt in response.

"Hang on, Devin." She shuffled through a stack of papers on the dining room table. An empty pack of cigarettes tumbled to the floor, scattering escaped tobacco remnants onto the carpet. "It's here somewhere."

I shifted my weight from one foot to the other. I didn't have any particular plans for the morning, but I was anxious to get going. "Can this wait?"

"Here it is," she said, holding up a creased sheet of Colgate letterhead.

"When did that come in?"

She ignored my question. "According to this letter, you have to spend six weeks this summer on campus to get immersed in the college lifestyle."

Six weeks! I couldn't believe it. I'd been counting down the days to orientation weekend since the acceptance letter came in the mail. Now I could leave even earlier. "When?"

"Dear Mr. Hughes," Mom mumbled as she scanned the letter, "college is a big transition ... prepare you for success ..."

"When is it?" I asked again. Mom gave me a warning look over the top of the paper. "Sorry."

She continued skimming. "Here it is. Second week of July."

I felt my cheeks stretch across my face before I even

realized I was grinning. I barely heard Mom fretting about having to take time off work. Deliverance was less than two weeks away.

Mom and I left a day before the letter told us to be there. Dad got up early and helped us pack Mom's Pontiac, but he had to work at the grocery store the next day, so he couldn't come with us.

"Good luck," he said with a big grin. He crushed me in a hug. "Remember, don't trust nobody!"

At first Mom and I sat in silence, the radio playing at a low hum in the background. The windows were cracked, and hot summer air blasted through the vents of the Fiero. I couldn't sit still. This was it—the start of my new life. The miles flew by as we sped down the yellow brick road to my own personal Emerald City.

"I'm going to miss you, Devin," Mom said.

At first I thought her words were part of my daydream. Visions of Division I basketball, cheerleaders, and toga parties danced in my head.

"I meant it. I'm proud of you."

I stared out the window. The rush of the outside world slowed to a halt as I tried to make this moment last a lifetime. I hardly dared to breathe, afraid that a sudden exhalation would blow back the curtain and reveal the charlatan masquerading as the great and powerful Oz. This had to be real.

"Make sure you focus on your work. You need to study."

"I know. I can handle school."

The Fiero drifted right as she looked over at me. "You have to stay away from the girls."

I rolled my eyes on the outside, but inwardly I ate up the attention.

"Don't give me that. I know how you are. You have to stay focused. Focused, focused, focused."

"Okay, okay. I got it." I didn't mind the sudden dose of parenting. She could've said anything just now; this was the first step in moving on with my life.

We pulled into the parking lot of the Colgate Inn just as the sun started to set. The old Dutch colonial glowed with the last light of the day. After Mom checked us into our room, we down to the tavern for dinner. Heavy wooden beams and simple black metal chandelier lighting gave the place a dark but earthy feel. When we finished our meals, Mom pushed her plate aside and lit up a cigarette. Her eyes shone.

"We've been through some tough times," Mom said. She exhaled a stream of wispy gray smoke. "You remember that ratty apartment in the city?"

How could I forget? I could still see the roaches skitter across the counter in my memory. "Yeah."

"And your dad, he's had some issues."

He wasn't the only one. I wanted to say something, but I realized the shine in her eyes was the glimmer of tears.

"He's had it rough, battling with the alcohol and his medication." The teardrops slid down her cheeks. She opened her mouth as if to say something else, but just took a quiet, shuddering breath.

"Mom, it's going to be fine." I didn't know what else to say. I didn't want to sit here and relive all the painful memories of my childhood; we were here so I could move on with life. "Everything is going to be fine. This is where we wanted to get to, remember?"

"I know, I know." She swiped the tears away with the palm of her hand and forced a smile.

That night, we sat in the lobby of the hotel for hours, talking and people watching. The other guests at the inn didn't really fit our demographic: a slew of the yuppie crowd passed through the doors while we sized them up. There were a few families with students, but most were the summer vacation crowd. Mom came alive, her eyes bright and responsive, her tongue sharp and on point. She giggled and smoked, sipped a cocktail, and had a great time. It was as though we were the only two people there. I hadn't seen her smile like that in years.

We set out bright and early the next morning. Mom wanted to get a look at the town and campus before she made the trek home. She kept up a stream of chatter as we drove through the streets of Hamilton. I couldn't tell whether it was the college chance she never had, or whether she was just excited for me, but it was as though she wanted to soak up as much of the experience as she could and take it back to DC in her suitcase. She parked at the curb outside a big gray house on Fraternity Row. Parents and students swarmed the front yard. We unloaded my things in the midst of the hubbub.

"Okay, Mom, I'm all set," I said, grabbing my last bag from the backseat.

"Don't you want to unpack? I could help."

"No, I'll be fine."

"Are you sure?" She crossed her arms and leaned against the car.

"Yeah, Mom, I'm sure."

"Well." She looked at me and fell into silence.

We stood there for a few long, awkward minutes, neither one of us speaking. She hadn't gone to college, so she didn't have any specific guidance to give me, but I could tell she didn't want to leave.

"Stay away from the girls, Devin," she said again, wagging a warning finger at me.

"I know. I have to stay focused."

Finally, after repeating all of the advice she'd given me in the car yesterday, she hugged me, got in the car, and drove away.

I waited until the Fiero was out of sight, and then walked back into the chaos of 100 Broad Street. This would be my home for the next six weeks while Colgate prepared my peers and me for the rigors of college study. The other students in the summer program were in my demographic sweet spot: ninety-five percent of the people milling about the hallways were black and Latino. A lone white girl drifted in the sea of color.

I found my room easily. My roommate had already been there and claimed one of the beds. Two beat-up suitcases and a backpack sat untouched on the bare mattress. I dropped my bags on the floor and sat on the other bed.

"Hey, there you are!" A tall black guy around my height—six foot four—came through the doorway. He offered me his hand. "Henry Alston, Orange, New Jersey."

"Devin Hughes, Washington DC."

"You get recruited for basketball, too?"

"Yeah. I played for St. John's."

"Cool. Come out here and meet some people. There are a couple guys down the hall, Rodney and Ray, that are here for football."

We hit it off right away. We had three to four class sessions every weekday, but only philosophy was for actual credit. The rest were primer courses designed to ease us into reading and writing in the academic setting. After our two morning classes we walked up the hill to eat lunch at the cafeteria, had another class in the afternoon, and did homework afterward. It wasn't as rigid as a regular college curriculum, but it was enough to get my feet wet.

I did enough to keep my head above water in the noncredit courses, but I took a real interest in philosophy. The ambiguity and problem solving spoke directly to my life experiences. The answer didn't ever jump right out of the text; the professor encouraged us to synthesize all the information and look for hidden meanings in everything. We read Plato, Socrates, all the big names.

I came to the conclusion that there were few absolutes in life, but a lot of gray. Jerome Balmuth, my philosophy professor, showed us how most of our quick judgments were based on pattern recognition. Everyone in the class viewed the world through our own unique prisms; our perceptions of the same experiences were refracted by previously held biases and assumptions, changing the way we each thought about a particular problem. I became conscious of my own thought patterns, and how my reactions were a by-product of my past and the people I hung out with. Under this assumption, not all white people were crackers, and they didn't all fit the dorky, can't-fight-or-play-ball stereotype. Girls weren't all hoes. I recognized that I had to grow out of viewing everyone around me in the static terms I had grown up with.

Even though I found philosophy intriguing and it made me determined to be more careful in my judgments of others, I didn't want to study. Typical freshman. Over the weekend, we worked out in the gym with some of the other basketball players, but the majority of the time, Henry and I hung out and enjoyed the autonomy of college.

Race didn't come up until the end of the first week. We lay in our beds late at night, talking and winding down. A warm breeze drifted through the open window.

"Hey, Dev," Henry asked.

"What?"

"I've been meaning to ask you this ..." He trailed off into silence.

I waited it out, watching shadows from the trees outside wave across the ceiling. The even rise and fall of Henry's breath was the only sound in the room. "What?" I finally asked.

"You got any black in you?"

"Yeah, below my belt, dude."

Henry laughed. "No, seriously."

"Seriously. My dad is black." I gave him the abridged version of my life story.

"I knew it, man! I could tell."

"How could you tell that?"

He yawned. "The way you talk. You remind me of this guy at home."

I smiled to myself. He knew I was down.

Mom's advice aside, I dated a Puerto Rican girl named Katherine; she was also part of the summer program. Hanging out with her was fun, and I felt comfortable and accepted in our new circle of friends, but would I still fit in when regular classes started in the fall? Most of us in the summer program belonged to a minority; Colgate was primarily white. Then again, part of me was white. Could I connect with that untouched half of my identity? Would I still have to carry the biracial card with me, or could I just be me?

Two weeks before the end of the summer program, Sigma Chi threw its annual summer frat party. There had been no drinking on campus until that point. Rodney, Ray, and Henry were excited about the booze and the girls. I still didn't understand the appeal of getting wasted, but this was an actual frat party, like in the movies; I couldn't resist the temptation.

We walked the half-mile to the Sigma Chi house with a group of girls. Sigma Chi was the only frat on top of the hill. Music thumped through the air, audible from a block away. Streams of students flocked toward the big stone house, following its siren call. Inside, chaos reigned. I followed Rodney, Ray, and Henry to the kitchen. A giant trash can of punch sat in the middle of the room, surrounded by a crowd of frat brothers. They handed us all plastic cups. My friends filled theirs and started to drink. I looked at the undulating surface of the bright red liquid.

"Dude," Henry said as he elbowed me in the side. "You have to try this."

All eyes turned toward me. It seemed relatively safe. I was happy. I trusted my friends. *I'll just take a couple sips to be social.* I filled my cup and took my first sip. It tasted like fruit punch, sweet and syrupy, nothing like what I'd imagined my dad's breed of alcohol tasting like. When I swallowed, heat rolled down my throat and pooled in my stomach. It was a new sensation.

I quickly forgot about my plan to take a few sips here and there. As I went back for my first refill, I thought maybe I could handle this drinking business after all. I didn't feel any different. Maybe I wouldn't turn into the silly, sloppy drunk my dad was.

Within an hour, all four of us were trashed.

Henry and I found a couch and sat around cracking up at nothing. Girls appeared from nowhere and disappeared again in a blur of light and sound. Time didn't exist. The world spun around me. After a while, it felt as though I was the one spinning around the world, and the centripetal force kept me pinned to the corner of the sofa. I didn't even realize Henry had disappeared along with Rodney and Ray. Bone-deep exhaustion settled in as I hauled myself up from the couch, leaning against the wall as I walked down the hall. That was where I stood, my balance precarious, when Henry came stumbling toward me.

"Hey," he said, laying a big, meaty hand on my shoulder to steady himself. "You should come upstairs." He was drunk, but to a far lesser degree than I was.

The words didn't even register. I closed my eyes and let my head fall against the wall.

"Snap out of it," he said, waving his hands in my face. "You've got to come upstairs. We're running a train on this girl."

"I don't care. I'm not going anywhere."

"Dude, she's hot. You got to get on this. She's passed out." He giggled.

"Man, stop messing with me." They were setting me up for a practical joke. I knew it. Why would three guys want to have sex with the same girl, *especially* if she was passed out? I tried to push away from the wall and immediately regretted it. My head felt three times its normal weight, and my equilibrium couldn't compensate for even the slightest movement. It was as if someone had taken out my brains and filled my skull cavity with bright red punch, and I could feel it slosh back and forth with every movement.

"I'm not playing around, dude," Henry said. "Serious. Ray's up there right now. Let's go."

My stomach lurched. "No way. I'm out of here." I stumbled on my way to the door, but I didn't fall. I walked the entire way back to 100 Broad Street by myself, puking every five minutes. Every time I vomited that awful red bile, I wondered why my friends weren't there to make sure I didn't get lost, or accidentally wander into the lake, or get caught by security. Somehow I made it into my bed, where I passed out cold.

The next thing I knew, our bedroom door banged open. Three state troopers and a canine unit filled our room with shouting and large-brimmed hats. *Did I do something?* Paranoia set in immediately, followed closely by a tympanic pounding in my skull and a shag-carpet feeling in my mouth. I frantically tried to recall the events of the night before, but there was a giant blur between getting to Sigma Chi and waking up in bed. Was getting drunk illegal?

The troopers stood over Henry's bed, one of them shaking him violently. "Get up! Out of bed. Hands where we can see them!"

Henry looked like hell. His eyes were bloodshot. "What's going on?" he croaked.

"Get your clothes on," one of the troopers yelled. "Let's go."

I lay still, my back against the wall. Any second now, the shoe would drop for me.

Henry panicked as he pulled on his pants. "Hey, you need to call my parents," he said to me.

Is this really happening? "What am I going to say?" I grabbed my blanket in both of my hands and pulled it up under my chin.

"I don't know. Tell them I had to go with these guys."

I peered at the troopers' badges, but I couldn't make out where they were from. No way was I going to ask them. If I made eye contact, they might decide to take me along just for fun.

The troopers took Henry, Rodney, and Ray outside. The house was in an uproar. No one knew what was going on. Finally one of the other football players who'd been at the party came down and told us what he'd heard.

The guys hadn't been trying to play a joke on me last night. They had gone upstairs and raped the girl, one right after the other. (She would go on to file a negligence suit against Colgate, Sigma Chi, and Best Brands Inc., a beer distributor, for ten million dollars, and the case forever changed the way fraternities worked at the university.) I never saw Henry, Rodney, or Ray again.

That experience left a sour aftertaste on the summer. Echoes of my father's words haunted me. "Don't be vulnerable," he always said. "Don't let your guard down." He was right. The first time I took a drink, look what happened. I didn't know what to think, what to feel. I felt bad for the guys, and I felt bad for the girl, but I didn't know who she was. Did she know who I was? Did she know I was at the party with them? Would she think I was part of it? And what if I *had* drunkenly followed the guys upstairs, thinking they were joking? I would have been associated with what had happened. Henry wouldn't have been the only one pulled from our room that morning. The idea that one decision could totally change your life had never been illustrated so clearly. As the program drew to a close, one thing was obvious: if I was going to carve out a better future, I had to surround myself with different people.

CHAPTER 18

UNDERCOVER

DAD DROPPED ME OFF AT SCHOOL FOR MY FIRST FULL SEMESTER AT COLGATE. He talked all the way up from DC. I half listened; I was excited about starting the real college experience, and looking forward to meeting the rest of the basketball team. In the back of my mind, I wondered whether I would fit in with the general student body. The weight of Dad's stare gave the sudden stillness a heavy air.

"Sorry, what was that?" I asked.

"I was just saying about that baseball team I used to coach when you were little."

"The Tigers?"

"Yeah. You've come a long way since then."

That's an understatement. My elementary school days felt eons ago.

"A long way," Dad repeated. "I'm proud of you, son. Who would've thought you'd come from that to get a quality education and play Division I basketball?"

"It's pretty cool," I said. I couldn't summon any enthusiasm for the conversation. I was ready to let it all go and start a new chapter in my life.

As we left the freeway, I started to get anxious about Dad causing a scene on campus. Colgate was a completely different world than what we knew. When the Buick rolled up to the curb outside my dorm, it was the only domestic model in the lot. BMWs and Saabs crowded the street. Affluent white women dressed to the nines checked their reflections in their tinted car windows and fussed over their children's clothing. Did their eyes linger a moment longer on Dad and me than on the other students? What were they thinking about a six-foot-four white kid and a five-foot-eleven black man wandering around campus together? Mom had her own issues, but at least we looked alike, and she fit the racial demographic a little better.

Dad didn't have any comments as he climbed out of the car. I did my best to seem inconspicuous in my athletic gear in the midst of a crowd dressed in preppy chic. We grabbed my bags and hauled them up to the third floor of East Hall. The room was right across the hall from the girls' bathroom; the guys' bathroom was at the other end of the building. My roommate hadn't arrived yet.

"You can just leave those on the bed," I said, dropping my own armload on the floor.

"So this is your place." Dad walked a lap around the tiny room. He sat on the edge of the bed. Out in the hallway voices shouted and hollered as new roommates greeted each other. I had to get Dad out of here.

"Well, I'm good," I said.

"You sure? Because I could—"

"No, I'm fine. Besides, you've got a long drive home." I couldn't quite meet his eye. "I'll walk you back out to the car." I saw no need to have Dad linger. I was ready to jump in the deep end and go for a swim.

Back at the Buick, Dad gave me a quick hug. "Knock 'em dead."

"Okay, Pops."

"Stay in touch," he said, his voice a little rough around the edges.

I promised I would, and we said good-bye. All told, Dad spent about fifteen minutes on campus before he turned around and went home. I felt a little guilty for treating him like a FedEx man whose only responsibility was to drop off the package—me—and leave, but I was anxious to do my own thing. As soon as the car disappeared from sight, I searched the dorms for people I knew from the summer program. Katherine flagged me down right off the bat and showed me her room. I took her back to see mine and served up a big culture shock to my new roommate.

Clint was from Texas. He had the start of a bald spot and a strong country accent in his soft voice. A small part of me immediately classified him as racist. A pot-luck roommate, he wasn't a student athlete, just someone I got stuck with according to the luck of the draw.

"Hi," I said. *He's definitely not going to be one of my boys.*

His eyes widened into two giant marbles as he stared up at me. "You're on the basketball team, right?"

"Right. I just stopped by to show Katherine the room. We're heading out to find some other people we know."

We hightailed it out of there, leaving Clint staring at our backs with those big round eyes. He'd called once over the summer and Mom had told him I was at "the club," meaning the gym. Poor Clint had assumed she meant country club. Somehow I didn't think my nylon shorts would meet the dress code.

Katherine and I walked over to the Harlem Renaissance Center, or HRC, which was where most of the students of color found their housing. Immediately on walking into their lounge, I felt on familiar ground. I scoped the place out, introduced myself to a few people, and had a few laughs. I couldn't help but think about Clint. He was definitely different. I didn't want to disown the black experiences that had brought me this far, but I wanted to know more about the other side.

Over the next few weeks, I paid attention to the differences between Colgate students and the people I knew back home. Even something as simple as the clothes I wore set me apart from other students. My daily outfit consisted of gym shorts and T-shirts. When I needed something nicer, I grabbed khaki shorts and a golf shirt to pair with my sneakers. All around campus, I saw labels I'd never heard of, like L.L. Bean and J. Crew. Every day I heard somebody mention which prep schools they had attended or ski vacations they'd gone on with their parents. I'd never heard of prep school, and I couldn't picture Mom taking on a bunny slope without a bong in her hand.

I turned to the basketball team to find a new social circle. Practice started in early October, but I played pickup games with a few guys starting in September. Through those initial games I met John Costello. He was a white kid from Boston who loved hoops and rap music. He was the first white person I'd met that liked rap. John was a basketball junkie. Unlike me, he'd made it into Colgate based purely on merit, and did a walk-on tryout for the team. We ended up spending most of our time together on the basketball court.

Our pre-Colgate lives could not have been more different. John's father was an orthodontist. He had a younger brother and sister, and the family owned two houses in Cape Cod, and sat down to nightly dinners with both parents. He was a perceptive guy; he noticed how fluidly I moved in and out of the black social circles, and that my basketball style was showier than your typical white kid. I never made an effort to conceal my father's race, so it wasn't long until everyone knew. John, naturally, was intrigued.

"What was it like, growing up like you did?" he asked while we practiced layups one day.

I looked at the basket, set up my shot, and let the ball fly. It bounced off the rim. "What do you mean?"

"You know, what was your 'hood' like?" His questions were innocent; the different perspectives we had on the world around us genuinely intrigued him. He quickly became my best friend both on and off the team.

During the first few months I talked to my parents at least once every two weeks. When my parents were lucid, all of our conversations sounded the same.

"How's the college man?" Dad's voice shouted from the other end of the line.

"Great. I love it here."

"Are you having any issues?"

"No, everything's fine."

"How's the coach—"

"Give me the phone, give it to me." Mom's voice was muffled in the background. "Are you studying?"

"Yeah, Mom."

"You better be working hard. Are you staying away from the girls?"

I thought of Suzanne. We lived on the same floor, were enrolled in the same major, and had a lot of classes together. She was a basketball player, too, a six-foot brunette with blue eyes. I saw her all the time, and she liked to tease me about my use of the girls' bathroom right across from my room. "Yep, I'm staying away," I lied.

"Good. You still like it there?"

"It's awesome. This is exactly where I want to be." That was the truth. Colgate provided that sense of order and stability I craved. Since the upheaval at the end of the summer program, I'd been careful about who I associated with at school.

One of the guys I'd met in the summer program came from a similar background as I did—athletics was our golden ticket into Colgate. Marcus Sellars lived in Rochester and had been recruited for the football team. We both depended on sports to keep us at the university; neither one of us had any other means of paying for tuition. The difference between rich kids and us was obvious.

I walked through "the Coop"—O'Connor Campus Center—willing myself not to look toward the mail slots. No matter how hard I tried not to, I checked every time I walked past, hoping to get something.

"Hey, check it out!" One of the guys from my floor pulled a brown paper parcel out of his mailbox. A small crowd of students gathered around him. Everyone celebrated care packages from home. Everyone who got one.

The lucky guy tore into the box amidst calls of "What's in it?" and "Dude, what did you get?"

I lingered on the edge of the crowd. What would it be like to come in one day and see one of those packages waiting for me?

He held up two brand new sweaters, probably L.L. Bean. "Nice! I can put off laundry another two days."

"What else is in there?" One of his buddies reached for the package.

"Hands off!" he said with a laugh. "My mom isn't sending this stuff for you."

"That's not what she said last night."

The room erupted with bawdy laughter. More treasures emerged from the package. Assorted boxes of candy and crackers bloomed from eager hands. A cellophane bag of popcorn rustled.

I tore myself away and shuffled toward the stairwell. Hoots and hollers drifted after me. There was always a check stuffed into the bottom of the packages. Even Marcus and I knew that. My eyes drifted involuntarily to my own empty mail slot. Secretly, I wanted a care package more than anything, but I never asked. I assumed it was out of my reach. As the semester wore on, my talks with my parents degenerated. Dad's mania crackled across the airwaves as clear as static. When Mom answered the phone, her voice drawled with drugs. Usually, I hung up the phone as quickly as possible. I didn't need any more reminders of my old life.

"Are your parents coming to town next weekend?" Suzanne asked that Friday. We were heading for the dining hall between classes. It was late October. Piles of leaves whirled and danced on the lawns around us.

"I don't think so." A chill rushed down my back. I hadn't told them Parents' Weekend was coming up. I wanted them to come so I could enjoy it like the rest of the student body, but no way could I invite my mom and dad. I wanted to fit in at Colgate. I rationalized my omission by telling myself that they might feel uncomfortable, but mostly I didn't want them compromising the new identity I'd built for myself. "How about yours?"

"I'm pretty sure they'll come," she said. She pushed a lock of brown hair behind her ear. A smile lit up her blue eyes. I felt the start of a crush creeping into my consciousness. "They've been talking about it for weeks."

The next week, a definite autumn chill lingered in the air. I stuffed my hands deep into my pockets and hunched my shoulders against the cold. By Friday afternoon, campus was flooded with families. Everywhere I looked, the senders of the care packages smiled proudly and hugged their students. The stands at that weekend's football game were crowded with a sea of maroon and white bought at the campus store earlier that day. I hung around with some of the other students whose parents didn't come. We all tried to stay busy to keep our minds off it. Everyone else went out to dinner with his or her parents. I didn't meet Suzanne's folks.

The weather turned colder. Washington DC wasn't that far away from Hamilton, but I wasn't prepared for the winter. All the guys on campus wore long, black overcoats. Two weeks ago I'd asked my parents for some money to buy a decent coat. The check they promised hadn't come. I wasn't surprised that I never received one. Disappointed, but not surprised. It wasn't the money—my parents were scattered, unfocused, and I was out of sight, out of mind. There was no malignant intent; buying me a coat just wasn't a priority in their minds. I'd managed a lot of things on my own for a while, so it wasn't the coat I wanted from them as much as some sense of normalcy and commitment.

I shivered all the way to basketball practice. Between the two hours of drills six days a week, plus an hour and a half of going to and from and watching tapes, it was a huge time commitment. I liked to compete, but I didn't like working at it. Coach Baker and I didn't have a great connection; it all added up to one big realization: I didn't have a love for the game. Instead of going to the gym, I turned around and went back to my room, where it was warm. That was the first, but not the last, time I skipped. I called my parents to remind them about the money for a coat.

"Hey, Pops."

"Devin! How's life on campus, college man?"

"Cold." I kept my voice calm and even. "Did you send the money yet?"

"Well, about that …"

"You didn't send it, did you?"

"We get paid on Friday."

"Are you going to remember to mail it this time?" I twisted the phone cord around my fingers.

"Of course."

"And you're sending one-fifty, right? It has to be enough for a good winter coat."

"You'll have it next week, don't worry about it," he promised for at least the third time.

"It's not going to bounce again, is it?"

Dad ignored that one. "I know it's cold. We'll get it."

When the check finally arrived, it was only for fifty dollars. Thankfully, my room and board were both already covered, or who knew when I would've eaten. I almost never asked my parents to send a certain amount; I just asked for whatever they could spare, but this was different. I skipped practice again, took my fifty bucks, and went to a thrift shop with Marcus to find a coat and some warmer winter clothes.

The musty secondhand smell assailed us as soon as the door opened. Dozens of cheap metal racks crowded the tiny shop. I pushed my way through the tangle of hangers, looking in vain for a castoff from last season. If all my classmates were wearing brand new coats, someone had to have turned in a relatively new one. The price tags were scribbled with sloppy, handwritten numbers. I grabbed a few things and added up the cost to see if I could afford them all or if I'd have to put something back.

The coat I settled on cost twenty dollars. It was fine— at home, this would have been a cool jacket, but here I was, a Division I university student, shopping for used clothes out of necessity while my classmates wore the best of the best. How could I assimilate into the affluent culture around me if I couldn't even afford to look like one of them? That coat was the capstone on the great divide between the white students and me. I never told my parents about the disappointment. By this point I wasn't studying, wasn't practicing. Instead, I went out with Suzanne and socialized with people on campus. I compartmentalized my feelings and focused on the things I enjoyed.

After a week of skipping practices, I had a bunch of unreturned calls from Coach Baker. Mom kept pushing until I finally agreed to talk to him.

My feet dragged all the way to Baker's office. It was like being sent to the principal's office. I dreaded this conversation. For the last two months I hadn't gotten any positive feedback from him, probably because I didn't deserve any. My game had no hustle, no drive. We aired it out over his desk. I realized I didn't want to quit the team, so I apologized and nodded at everything he said. He didn't tell me anything that changed my feelings; I still didn't love it, but I did enjoy the camaraderie of the team, and it was my ticket to stay. If I wasn't a hoop player, then what was I? I was an average student in Vanillaville.

Studying was a foreign concept. As usual, I did the bare minimum I needed to squeak through my classes. I just didn't care. I met a couple of other student athletes, and they became my core group of friends. David Goodwin and Jeff Lynch played on the football team. Matt Kolber played JV basketball. We hung out regularly, but I also cast my net wider. I went to any frat party, any social gathering, anything that exposed me to other people; I was a social butterfly.

Even though I looked the part and acted the part, I couldn't force myself completely into the white mold. The very first time I remembered feeling uncomfortable about race was at a frat party between Thanksgiving and Christmas break. At Colgate, there were white parties, and there were black parties; the only black students who came to white parties were athletes. This particular night was a white party. I stood around with a group of guys from my dorm, nursing a plastic cup of beer. A group of guys from my Intro to Psych class stood maybe ten feet away, holding mixed drinks. They looked like they'd stepped right out of the Colgate college brochure with their khakis and J. Crew sweaters. They laughed their asses off, drawing my attention like a bug to flypaper.

"Did you see her walk into class yesterday?" one of them asked.

"Who?"

"You know, the booga bear."

Booga bear? I couldn't have just heard that. The guys kept joking back and forth about her. It was as though all other sound had been sucked out of the room and all I could hear was their braying laughter. I knew immediately what girl they were talking about—there was only one black girl in that lecture class.

I wanted to march over and give them a lesson, a sermon, maybe just a punch in the face. Everyone at the party was white. Everyone. I was trying to fit in.

My mind spiraled into turmoil, but I outwardly shrugged it off. The last thing I needed was to get tossed out of school for fighting. After that comment, I felt so awkward I left the party. I'd had the opportunity to educate these clowns, but I walked away. Was I a sellout? Or were all white people racist at heart? Once again I found myself torn between two polar opposites. I desperately wanted to connect to the white world, but incidents like this derailed me.

By Valentine's Day, I had gathered up the courage to send Suzanne a card. I picked one out of the rack at random, scrawled "*Love, Devin,*" on the inside, and sent it through the campus mail system. She didn't talk to me for a week. It was torture. She was bright, smart, attractive, wholesome, and athletic; she was all the adjectives that I had always wanted to find in a girl. When I finally got her to talk to me, we sat near one of the big windows on our floor.

I took a deep breath. "I want you to be my girlfriend."

She looked at me as if I were crazy. "I need to think about that."

I was crushed. The first time I officially asked someone to be my girlfriend, and she blew me off.

"Just give me a week," she said. "We're such good friends. I don't want to ruin it."

A few days later she said yes. We kept it a secret from other people. Our reasoning was that we didn't want people on the floor to feel uncomfortable and not want to hang out with us. We hung out a lot, did everything together, but didn't publicize it. During that time we learned each other's nuances. This was an entirely new way of relating to women for me, and she could tell.

"You're too flirty," she told me one day in a huff.

"What are you talking about?"

"You know what I'm talking about." Her blue eyes blazed with irritation. "The way you talk to girls. You're too friendly."

We argued about how I dealt with other girls a few times, but for the most part we had smooth sailing. She kept me grounded. It felt like a real college experience.

"What are you doing?" she asked when she swung by my room unannounced.

I looked up from the TV. "Nothing."

She walked over to the set and turned it off. "You're supposed to be working on your paper."

"I'll get around to it."

"Devin, it's due Friday. We've had the assignment for six weeks. You have to go do your research."

"All right, all right. You coming to the library with me?" I grinned at her.

She looked as if she wanted to be mad, but she couldn't help but smile. "If that'll get you to do your assignment, let's go."

When our relationship became more serious, my struggle with my identity came to the forefront again.

"Do your parents know about my background?" We sat at a small restaurant in downtown Hamilton, waiting for our order, when I asked that million-dollar question.

"I've honestly never thought about it," she said. She looked out the window. Outside, the last traces of snow were melting, rivulets of dirty water trickling toward the sewers.

"Well?" I asked.

"Well, what?"

"Do you think they'd care that my dad is black?"

Suzanne didn't answer right away. Her hesitation unnerved me. Kelley, the white girl I'd dated in high school, used to tell me all the time how prejudiced her father was. I was genuinely concerned about what Suzanne's parents would think. I'd spent a year distancing myself from that part of my life, but would other people be able to see past where I'd come from? Or would their opinions of me forever be predetermined by something I couldn't control?

CHAPTER 19

SOCIAL PROOF

FRESHMAN YEAR FLEW BY, AND ALTHOUGH I HAD A BLAST SOCIALLY, I STILL NEVER FELT LIKE I FIT IN.

I was in no rush to hang out with the minority crowd, and I didn't want to pretend I belonged with the preppy crowd, either. I spent a lot of time hanging out with upperclassmen, athletes, frat boys, and a variety of groups, just trying to figure out the best place for me in Colgate's vast and homogenous ecosystem.

Toward the end of freshman year, I was tired of feeling isolated because of my mixed race. I was no academic superstar, but what I was learning in school had a profound effect on me; I started peeling back the onion of my own behavior, trying to figure out why I thought, felt, and acted the way I did. I couldn't help but wonder whether my experiences would be different if I viewed them through a different perspective.

It wasn't necessary for me to bring up my racial identity, but I felt better having it out there than feeling as though I had to be on guard lest someone find out the wrong way. Thus, any time the topic steered toward what my parents did or where I came from, I took the opportunity to experiment. Then, like a social scientist, I made detailed observations about people's reactions.

"Well, my background is probably a lot different than yours," I told a guy from my dorm one day. We sat at a table at the Coop drinking sodas between classes. My partner was a typical Colgate kid: white, with parents footing the bill for tuition.

"Oh, yeah? How's that?" He eyed the instructions for our next assignment.

"I went to a military school in inner-city Washington

DC." I watched his reactions carefully. So far, nothing. "And I'm mixed, so that gives me a different perspective."

My lab partner's forehead wrinkled. Time stopped for a few seconds while he processed the information. We sat there and stared at each other, two human beings both fully capable of communicating in English, yet neither one knowing what to say to end the awkward moment.

He finally found his voice. "Really?"

"Yeah, my dad is black."

"Huh. I never would have guessed."

Most people reacted that way. A few here and there looked triumphant and said, "I thought so." No one ever reacted negatively—at least not to my face. Then again, I was over six feet tall, weighed two-twenty, and had a bit of an edge; I doubt anyone would have expressed racist remarks even if they had them. Things might have been different if I had gone to school in Mississippi.

I spent a lot of time that year trying to understand why I felt so uncomfortable around white people, as though they were always judging me. Why was it that any time two white people looked in my direction, I made assumptions about what they were saying about me? Did this reflect *actual* reality, or was I simply dragging all of Dad's baggage along behind me? The more I thought about it, the more it made sense that I was seeing things not as *they* were, but as *I* was. Maybe, instead of worrying about what everyone else thought, I should work on making myself the person I wanted to be.

At the end of my freshman year, I had to figure out where I was going to live next fall. I got along with Clint, but I didn't want to live with him again, and I didn't want to get stuck with another random person. I didn't have a strong desire to join a frat; besides all the goofy rituals and groupthink, I wasn't sure how I would fit in. John pushed me to pledge with him. The guys I'd stayed with on my first campus visit were members of Kappa Delta Rho, a football, basketball, and swimming fraternity. Between Jim, Tony, and John's encouragement, I got caught up in the enthusiasm. We met with a few of the guys, and the kinship and brotherhood inside the KDR house was what finally convinced me to join. Rush week wasn't particularly memorable, except for Hell Night.

"Hell Night is a rite of passage for all new KDRs," John said as we hustled down the sidewalk to the frat house. Initiation started promptly at seven. We'd been warned not to be late. Normally, lights shone from every window of the house, and the building took on the life and energy of those inside, becoming a living, breathing entity of its own. Tonight, it loomed dark and silent, a mausoleum in which to inter our freshman-year experiences.

The front door swung open before we could knock, and one of the brothers greeted us with a raised hand. He wore a grave expression. An air of solemnity washed over me as we stepped inside.

"This way," he said in a deep voice.

We followed him down creaking wooden steps into a dark basement. At the bottom of the stairs, I could see faintly flickering light, but I had to feel my way down the steps blindly. John walked in front of me. Nervous energy radiated from him with every step he took.

"Play it cool, man," I said to him quietly.

"No talking," our guide snapped.

John flinched. I almost laughed out loud.

At the bottom of the stairs we were shown into a room where the other pledges already waited. Our guide left. We sat in the dark, tense, waiting for something to happen.

"Kneel, pledges," a commanding voice boomed at us from the back of the room.

I fell in line between John and another fidgety freshman. I turned my head to the left and right, watching the guys around me. *Is this supposed to be intimidating?* These were guys we saw every day. *I'll play along until somebody tries to humiliate me.*

A master of ceremonies appeared before us. He droned on in what I assumed was supposed to be an ominous monotone, designed to move its listeners to fear. What a joke. This guy was no Louis Farrakhan, but the rest of the pledges fell for the spiel anyway. He rambled a bunch of lines we were supposed to repeat. I bit my lip.

"Gentlemen, it's time for you to prove yourselves worthy."

All around us, the brothers began to chant. They herded us up the stairs into the house. Every room was set up to be a different trial.

"On your knees, boys!" the brothers yelled. "Now crawl! Crawl like the lowlife scum you are!" We dropped to the ground and bumped and scrabbled our way across the kitchen and into the living room. Pitchers of water hailed down on us while the litany continued. In one room, a group of KDRs stood in a circle and pushed a pledge around like an oversized footbag in a game of Hacky Sack, screaming at him all the while.

"Who do you think you are?"

"Why should we let you in?"

"Are you good enough?"

This was nonsense. Compared to some of the things I had been through in my childhood, the whole ritual felt completely hokey. Nothing but theater. I played along, stuck with John, and got to the end of it.

The ceremony ended with us repeating the credo. We were wet and bedraggled, but really no worse for wear.

The room buzzed with a low hum of voices, like a prayer in church where everyone says the words without thinking about the meaning. I repeated all the words given to us. None of the pledges were turned away, so John and I were both accepted. That solved the question of where I'd live in the fall, but off-campus housing meant I needed a car. No way was I going to walk to campus every day in the winter. That gave me one mission over the summer: save up enough money to buy myself a Jeep.

When I got home to DC, it was as if time had stood still when I left, waiting for me to come back and start the clock again. I had no interest in spending time within the four walls of our townhouse; I wanted to keep pushing forward, continue the momentum I'd been building toward a path of success.

The day after I came home, I interviewed for a job at a department store at the local mall. I didn't tell anyone about my background. These people had no idea who I was, where I came from, or where I was going, but they put me on the cleaning crew with a bunch of grown black and Latino men. Talk about judging a book by its cover. I didn't care; it was an easy, mindless job, and it got me out of the house.

The store was like its own little ecosystem, with clear divisions between the echelons of employees. Everyone looked down on the trash crew. Our job was to roll around the store with giant plastic garbage carts and pick up detritus. Salesclerks, especially, seemed to think they were better than us, as though standing behind a counter hawking jewelry or perfume meant they owned it.

"Hey," one of the men at the watch counter said, snapping his fingers.

I looked over. My shift had just started.

"Go pick that up," he said. He pointed at a crumpled receipt ten feet away from where I was emptying the trash can behind a case of earrings.

What is this, a plantation? I didn't say anything, just shrugged and picked up the paper. I would've gotten to it soon enough, anyway.

A mom hustled past with a big shopping bag clutched in one hand and an expensive purse gripped tightly in the other. Her eyes passed right over me, as if I didn't exist. A four-year-old dawdled along behind her. The little boy stopped to stare at my trash cart.

"Hi," I said. I smiled down at him.

"What's that thing?" he asked, pointing a chubby finger at the cart.

I was about to answer when the mother came back and grabbed his hand. "Come on, Brady. Get away from there." She dragged him away without ever making eye contact with me. Just because I picked up trash didn't make me a deviant, but that was the way we were treated in the store.

Assimilating to the group of cleaners felt natural. It was like putting on an old pair of shoes that I hadn't worn for a while. I was on the daytime crew with a half dozen other guys. The store manager talked down to us during every daily meeting.

We all met at the back of the warehouse at the beginning of our shift. The manager sat while the rest of us stood; other than mine, his was the only white face in the bunch.

"You guys got to get off of your lazy asses and work harder." He leaned back in his chair, high and mighty, never making real eye contact with any of us. "We got too much trash in this store."

The seven of us stood there, the newer employees taken aback by his harsh tone of voice. A couple of the guys were Puerto Rican. They both had children and wives at home. They had to take this guy's abuse because this was their only job and they didn't want to get fired.

The manager continued his diatribe. "You people are complaining that the trash is filling up, but you got to stop goofing around. What are you guys thinking?"

You clown, I thought. *When I graduate, you'll be working for me.* I couldn't believe the company had this white guy treating his crews like three-year-olds. Was this how Dad felt every day at the A&P?

He railed at us for ten minutes, then turned us loose with another warning to stop goofing around. We all walked away feeling downtrodden.

"That asshole," one of the new guys said. "He doesn't get it."

"He doesn't respect us," one of the seasoned guys on the crew said. He shook his head.

It was sad to hear all the negativity after those meetings; I could tell the manager's words stung them, when all they wanted was some affirmation that they were doing a good job. I stuck around because I wanted that Jeep at the end of the summer. Once I had those keys in hand, there was no way I'd let myself be put in this kind of situation again. Most of the other guys didn't have the same kind of end in sight.

The store was like a lab that simulated the whole outside world as a social experiment. I never wanted people to feel the way we all felt working for this manager; I wanted to be a source of inspiration, to make people feel like they were a part of something bigger. The few times I had one-on-one conversations with the manager, I exacted revenge in my own small way.

Our crew had set processes and routines for going about the daily grind; one of those was that we always started in the shoe section, then moved on around the jewelry cases. After the next morning's meeting, I elbowed one of my coworkers in the side just before our boss turned us loose.

"Hey, watch this," I murmured. I turned to the manager and cleared my throat. "Hey, I'm curious. Is there a reason why we start in shoes?" I kept the tone of my voice light and innocent; I didn't give him any reason to think I was being sarcastic.

"Huh?" He scratched his head.

"Is there something significant about the shoe area?"

"Uh, well, what do you mean?" The gears in his head ground to a halt. He was used to feeling like the smartest guy in the room; someone asking questions, especially using better-than-average vocabulary, unnerved him.

"Is there something specific about the trash in the shoe area that requires attention before the trash in the jewelry area?"

He gave me an odd look. He couldn't tell whether I was kidding.

I didn't do it every day, but any time he sat down and tried to punish us with his language, I found a way to make him uncomfortable, box him in. I put him in a precarious position where he wasn't the biggest, he wasn't the smartest, and he wasn't in control. On some level I wanted to make him feel the way he made the rest of the crew feel, but I don't think he ever connected those dots.

After my shift at the department store, I borrowed one of my parents' cars and spent another six hours delivering pizza for Godfather's. I worked from seven in the morning to eleven at night every day, and I dug in and performed top-notch at both jobs. The difference between these and the ones I'd been fired from all through high school was that I had a tangible goal I was working toward; I wanted that Jeep.

Whether it was sports, schoolwork, or even friendships, if I wanted something, I would fight, scratch, and claw for it. Every day, I woke up with that goal in mind, thinking of ways I could achieve it. The daily grind didn't bother me, because I felt as if I were on the path to something better. When I found myself thinking negatively, I used the power of self-talk to push me through; my thoughts ran through a constant good-cop/bad-cop routine on every shift.

After my shift at Godfather's ended, I'd go to the track at eleven in the evening and run. Even though I didn't play much ball that summer, I wanted to stay in shape; I wanted to make my sophomore year a good year on the courts, prove to myself that I could be on my A-game all the time.

I didn't interact with my parents much that summer, nor did I connect with any of the guys I'd played with at St. John's. I had cut the cord there, much like what my parents had done a number of times throughout my childhood—their families, Lela. Moving forward without looking back was part of the baggage I inherited with the Hughes name. The only person I had consistent contact with that summer was Suzanne.

Suzanne lived in Connecticut. Even though she was in a different state, I talked to her every day, sometimes for five minutes between deliveries at Godfather's, or for an hour or so late at night after dinner.

"How was your day?" I asked. I lay down on my bed and tried to untangle the knots in the phone cord with my free hand.

"Fine, I guess."

"Anything exciting happen?"

"In the last six hours? Ha ha, Devin."

I could picture the complete lack of enthusiasm on her face. "Hey, I have to ask. One of these days something will, and then you'll be mad that I don't ask."

"I'm just so ready for the summer to be over," she said.

I thought of dealing with the manager at the department store in the morning. "That makes two of us."

"I miss you."

"Yeah. Me too." I meant it.

Suzanne had everything that I didn't have. She came from a traditional, stable family. I hadn't met them yet, but she had a brother and a sister. Her parents wrote letters, called, had good jobs; all in all, they seemed pretty normal—Brady Bunch, even. By Colgate standards, they weren't particularly affluent, but they were definitely a step above my family. And Suzanne and I were friends. She was the first person in my life that I didn't want to walk away from.

By the end of the summer, I had saved several thousand dollars—more than enough to buy a secondhand Jeep. I found a CJ7 soft top listed in the classifieds and went to check it out. The royal blue paint job gleamed in the sunlight. My reflection bounced back at me off the chrome rims in the giant tires. It was perfect. With no hesitation, I handed over my few months' wages and accepted a pair of keys in return. I was amazed at how easy it was to accomplish my goal just by believing that I could, and sticking out jobs because they were a means to an end.

Buying that car represented freedom; I could come and go from Colgate whenever I wanted, I was taking on more responsibility, and it would help me assimilate with the rest of the students. All throughout freshman year, I had seen kids driving around in cars more expensive than anything my parents had ever owned, so for me, the Jeep was a big step forward.

As fall approached, bringing a familiar coolness to the air, I felt proud of my accomplishment and excited about what my second year at Colgate would bring. I no longer felt like I was heading into the unknown. Instead, I cruised down the highway with the top of the Jeep open, the wind blowing through my hair. I was on my way.

CHAPTER 20

THE OTHER HALF

FROM THE MOMENT I STEPPED OUT OF THE JEEP AND ONTO THE LAWN OF THE KDR HOUSE THAT FALL, I had

a lot more confidence. Mentally, I was much more prepared for what lay ahead of me. I was ready for the grind everywhere except the classroom.

"Hey, Tello," I called out to John, who was carrying a laundry basket stuffed with neatly folded clothes into the front door. From the bronze tone of his skin, I figured he'd spent the entire summer on the beach. "Wait up." I grabbed my bags and jogged to catch him.

"Nice wheels," he whistled. "That yours?"

"Worked all summer to buy it." I grinned. "How was your vacation?"

He shrugged. "Same as usual. Spent most of my time at the Cape with my family."

I held open the front door and let John pass me. "You check out the room yet?"

"Yeah. Jeff Lynch, John Gioffre, and Matt Kolber are all upstairs right now."

Jeff, John, and Matt were brothers at Delta Upsilon, a football fraternity one house down from KDR. We trudged up the creaking staircase. Half a dozen frat brothers careened down the steps in the opposite direction. The house felt alive with shouts and laughter. Halfway down the hall, I heard rap music thumping from the room John pointed out as ours.

"I'm not the only Wu-Tang fan," John said with a grin.

He introduced me to the other guys when we walked into the room. Three white faces greeted me. Three white hands shook mine. The frats were about as diverse as the rest of Colgate.

Suzanne and I saw each other regularly as well. New York Pizzeria in downtown Hamilton was one of our favorite haunts. I picked her up in the Jeep and drove us into town. The smell of bubbling mozzarella and toasted garlic wafted from the ovens no matter what time of day we went.

"Two slices of cheese pizza and a soda," I told the guy behind the counter.

"When's your first preseason workout?" Suzanne asked as we watched the freshly baked pizza slide onto the counter. Four quick cuts across the face of the pie later we each held a slice of the mouthwatering goodness and a stack of napkins in our hands.

I handed over my three dollars and we headed for a seat at the back of the shop. "Not until next week. Yours?"

"Same." She scooted into a booth and tucked her hair behind her ears. She looked just the way I remembered her—better, even. "What do you think of your chances this year?"

"I don't know. I don't have a good read on Baker."

"No? But I thought you said it was going okay at the end of last season."

"He's stale toast." I took a big bite of pizza. It burned the roof of my mouth.

"Stale toast?" Suzanne's eyebrows knitted together in a puzzled frown.

"Doesn't taste good, but if you're starving, you don't throw it out." I gulped soda to subdue the oily burn of the pizza. "I'm starving. So I'm going to try."

"What, you don't like the sidelines?" she teased.

"You're hilarious."

She blew on her slice to cool it, and then took a tiny bite off the end. "How about the team? Do you think you'll do better this year?"

I shrugged and changed the subject. "Hey, do you want to go to the DU party this Friday?"

"We don't have an early workout on Saturday, so why not?"

Between classes and practice, neither one of us had a lot of spare time, but we did manage to find time to spend together. We hung out between classes, went to frat parties on the weekends, and hung out and watched TV if we had any free time during the week.

I met her parents after one of her basketball games that fall. Her mom and dad took us out for dinner afterward.

Her dad was my height, and Irish. He was straitlaced, well mannered, spoke articulately, and presented a proper image. Suzanne's mother was an all-around nice, pleasant woman. Together, they made a happy couple sitting across the table from us.

I didn't hear half of what they said over dinner. *Man, if my parents were here, too, this would be a disaster.* My parents were so different I couldn't even begin to compare them. Dad meant well, but he was liable to weave some Malcolm X into the conversation and then drop an F-bomb on top for good measure. Somehow I couldn't make that fit with the Brady Bunch parents sitting across from me.

Both her parents sized me up all throughout dinner. Suzanne had told them about my background before we met, so instead of listening to them, I sat and wondered what they were thinking. Did they care that I was mixed? Did it bother them? If it did, they didn't show it.

"So," her dad said to me after we'd gotten some of the pleasantries out of the way. "How are your parents, Devin?"

"Oh, they're fine, thanks."

"What do they do?"

"They work a lot." I changed the topic as quickly as possible. "So, tell me about Suzanne," I said, looking at her with a smile. "When did she first start playing basketball?"

When Suzanne met my parents, it was a completely different picture. My mom was cold and rude from the beginning. Dad, of course, was the exact opposite; he was corny and laughing and saying all kinds of crazy stuff. I felt uncomfortable for Suzanne because I knew it was awkward. I tried to make everything come together, but Mom resisted every attempt at making civil conversation.

"It's not you," I assured an anxious Suzanne afterward. "Trust me—it's all her."

When Suzanne wasn't available, I hung out with John. Early in the semester we decided to take the Jeep for a road trip and stay at his parents' summerhouse in Cape Cod for a weekend. The house was right on the beach, so close to the water it could have had a dock leading right up to the back door. Cedar siding gave it an earthy, practical feel. The house itself wasn't ostentatious. I pulled the Jeep into the driveway and sat staring at everything. A basketball hoop loomed over us on the left side of the drive. The edge of a deck and a grassy backyard peeked out behind the corner of the house. The gentle roll of waves sounded like it came from the house itself.

"Holy shit, dude. This is your *second* house?"

John smiled. "This is it."

"This is awesome. We should come here for the summer."

"It's usually me and my mom. The rest of the family come and goes these days, but when I was younger all of us would be out here all summer."

This was more than a house. This was a retreat for the whole family. *I am going to have one of these one day.*

Between Suzanne and hanging out with my frat brothers, my social calendar was full; no matter what the function, I was there. Drinking wasn't a big pastime—I was in the party scene to meet new people, not to get ripped. Ever since that first party on the hill, I'd hated hangovers. I didn't understand how anyone could go out and drink to get drunk multiple nights a week and wake up feeling like their skull was two sizes too small for their brain. The majority of people I met were white. On and off campus, students of color lived together, and hung out and partied where they lived; there wasn't a lot of mixing, even at the bars downtown. I don't know if they didn't feel welcome at frat parties, but they isolated themselves from the white student body. My frat brothers became the basis of my new social circle; I didn't want my college experience to be an extension of high school, so I made an effort to mingle with the white students.

The only place where students of all colors really came together was on the athletic teams. My freshman year had been a bust on the courts, a complete waste of time. Sophomore year I wanted redemption. I had to prove that I had a lot more game than what I had presented. Three months of running the track after my pizza delivery job and squeezing in push-ups on my breaks at the department store ensured that I was more physically fit this time around. My technical skills were fine, but I'd graduated from the small pond of high school basketball to swimming with a lot of other big fish in Division I. It was time to dig deep.

The real season got into swing the week before Thanksgiving. I attacked every practice with a new attitude. Instead of keeping one eye on the clock and one on the net, I focused during every shooting drill. By half an hour into each practice, my jersey stuck to my skin with sweat. I stood in line for the water fountains with the rest of the guys, my lungs heaving just as hard as everyone else's.

The guy behind me clapped a hand on my shoulder. "Devin, did you have your Wheaties this morning or something?"

"Yeah, man, you are playing really well this year. Keep it up. Maybe we'll win a game."

I laughed with the rest of them. Bringing my best to the court every day felt great, but as a team our performance was still abysmal. We met the school's low expectation of men's basketball by losing our first four games in a row. The program hadn't had a successful year in so long that the team suffered from a loser culture.

It was the exact opposite of my high school team.

In high school, it was more than just the expectation of victory; we as players formed a deep connection with each other that carried us through four years of winning streaks. Here, I spent a lot of time chasing that orange ball up and down the court with my teammates, but out of bounds the friendships were cliquey. Everyone had his own agenda, including Coach Baker. He was a mannequin with a whistle as far as his players were concerned, a wannabe drill sergeant who lost his troops at the first order. No one could relate to him; he didn't demonstrate a broader vision and seemed uncomfortable letting his guard down to let his players get to know him. We were a team of Patty Hearsts, except that the brainwashing didn't stick: we all showed up, did our thing, and then went our separate ways at the sound of the buzzer.

Suzanne came to all the home games she could despite our poor record. She was one of the few dedicated fans who watched the opposing teams mop the floor with us all the way to the bitter end. The women's team wasn't having a stellar year, either. None of our games attracted much of a crowd. Often, she would wait for me outside the gym.

"Tough game tonight," she said when I walked out of the locker room. She gave me a quick hug.

"Now there's an understatement." We'd lost before the second half even started, and we knew it.

"A couple of the guys have been talking about you, though."

"Yeah?"

She smiled at me. "They say you seem really dialed in this year."

The positive affirmation made me grin with pride. I could feel it in myself. I was faster, stronger, in much better shape, and I had something to prove; I wasn't going to let my dad, the team, or myself down anymore. Freshman year was a fluke. This was the real me.

My parents never came to my games. They were too far away, even for home games. Dad coached me through some of the rough patches when I wanted to quit the team, and through the struggle of turning myself into a new player.

"Hang in there, Devin. Work through the challenges. If you give it your best shot, that's all anyone can ask."

His advice hit home on the basketball team, but I didn't translate that to my academic pursuits. My grades were atrocious, and I couldn't have cared less. From a workload standpoint I didn't have an especially grueling schedule. I took four classes per semester, just like the previous year, but the work was more challenging. I hadn't developed great study habits, and there were just too many extracurricular activities to distract me and fill the small gaps in my free time. Without someone to hold me accountable, I spiraled further and further toward academic probation.

Living in the frat house was not conducive to studying. With the rigorous physical effort I now poured into practice I was always tired. I did go to most of my classes, but I was just a body in a chair. Even though I couldn't recall anything the professors said five minutes after the bell set us free, I never acknowledged the fact that I had completely disengaged from my academic career. Fear of failing didn't even cross my mind.

After freshman year I had so much baggage regarding my racial identify, my nickname could have been Samsonite. Even though I looked as if I fit in with my roommates, I still felt different. That didn't go away but it also never came up with the guys in my circle. My racism radar was always on; I bucketed white people into one of two categories: color blind or bigoted. The more I hung out with my core group, the more I started to let go of my own preconceived ideas about white people.

By the time second semester rolled around, my hard work started to pay off on the team, and my lack of effort in the classroom came to its epoch. John came back from the campus bookstore with an armload of heavy books the Friday before classes resumed. He dropped them all on his bed and gave me a quizzical look.

"Dude, the bookstore's closing in twenty minutes. Shouldn't you go buy your texts before next week?"

I shrugged. "I'm not going to read them anyway. What's the point?"

When it came time for exams, I relied on the old habits I'd acquired from when I hid the fact that I couldn't read. I scrounged notes from anyone who was willing to share and memorized copious amounts of information, all of which I promptly forgot as soon as the exams were finished. In the days leading up to a test, I quizzed the people around me, asking them what they thought would be on the test or how they planned to study. Any piece of information I could suck out of my classmates, I did. Somehow, I scraped by.

Basketball was a completely different story. I was nowhere near the starting lineup—I was the seventh man in—but my primary objective during most practices was to play against the first team. Under normal circumstances, playing the second- and third-stringers gave the first team a good workout, but not always a tough challenge.

An even mix of maroon and white jerseys stampeded from one end of the gym to the other. The starters wore red jerseys. A crowd of white jerseys watched from the sidelines. Half the guys showed up to practice hungover or still drunk. One or two had thrown up in the trash cans between drills. I watched the ball bounce off the rim of my team's basket. The man I guarded jumped for the rebound, but I jumped just a little higher. My fingertips brushed the nubby leather. The ball came down toward me as my feet hit the ground. Elbows out to block my opponent, I looked for an opening. A white jersey ran in for a screen and I took off toward the other end of the gym. I passed the ball up to another teammate, who ran up for a textbook layup. Score. Our team beat the starters that day. I dominated the rebound count and I actually played defense. I was on fire.

Coach Baker stopped me on my way out of the gym. "Hughes, I want to talk to you a minute."

Immediately I was on guard. Baker was a dictator in the gym; I expected bad news. "What's going on?"

"I want you to wear the maroon jersey tomorrow."

"Coach?" I could hardly believe my ears.

"Not for good," he said. "We're just going to try you out."

From that point on, it was a gradual progression. Sometimes I wore red, sometimes white. By that point in the season, the coach was willing to try anything. He shuffled us around without a second thought to the starters he cut, or what he was doing to the fabric of the team. I had demonstrated a drive to succeed, where some of the other players weren't taking it as seriously. Everyone was tired of losing. In January I started five games. It didn't help our record, but getting better and gaining more playing time was its own reward.

In March we'd only won a grand total of five games all season. None of us had connected with Coach Baker in the first place, but as we continued to lose, he detached himself from his players. During a scrimmage, our collective frustration came to a head.

Tony Horne, one of the guys I'd roomed with during my first visit at Colgate, ran down the court after a botched play. We all congregated under the basket, awaiting direction from Baker. It was a white-jersey day for me, and I stood on the edge of the crowd. The coach had just started talking. Damp heat radiated from Tony's skin when he jogged up behind me, and his frustration was palpable. His mouthpiece made a wet, sucking sound as he peeled it off his teeth. A long strand of saliva drooped from his lip.

"Damn it to hell," Tony cussed. He threw the mouthpiece against the wall.

Coach Baker stopped in the middle of his sentence. He glared at Tony for a few long moments. He didn't tolerate outbursts from his players. An uneasy feeling settled over the team. Tony was a good guy, one of the players everybody liked. Baker stopped glaring, but the foreboding sensation remained. The next day Tony didn't show up for practice. He'd been kicked off the team.

Our already low morale sank even further. None of us thought Tony deserved to be dropped from the team for one frustrated outburst. On top of that, of course, Coach Baker never made us feel like we were part of something special. With him, it was like we were all in line at the DMV, waiting for our number to be called. The players turned against him, condemning him as a loser. We won a total of six games. He was fired at the end of the season.

When spring semester closed, my GPA had sunk to the low twos. I wasn't failing any of my classes, but I coasting by on the edge of the razor blade. I had no foresight at all about life after college. I never thought in those terms. To me, receiving the degree would lay out a world of opportunities at my feet. The mystery fairy would leave a pile of great jobs under my pillow at night. I didn't bother looking for internships. Life after college wasn't on my radar, and my parents didn't know what that looked like on the other side. They had no context for how that process worked or what would happen, so they couldn't help me. Their lives were on the same track as when I'd left in the fall. I knew I couldn't spend another summer in their house.

"What did your parents say about me spending the summer with you all?" I asked John. Plan A was to tag along to his place in Cape Cod.

John looked down. "Well, they aren't going to be around a lot."

"And that's a problem?" I laughed, trying to make the situation less uncomfortable.

"They don't want to be responsible if anything were to happen."

I shrugged it off. Okay … Plan B: one of Suzanne's friends from the women's basketball team had connections that would rent us a house just a few miles from the beach. We recruited Matt and three other girls. One thousand dollars apiece would get us all a nice place to stay, and I wouldn't have to worry about whether my dad was off his medication or how much Mom was self-medicating.

During the day I found a summer league that played pickup ball. Running up and down the court in the hot sun was way better than picking up trash in a windowless department store. I wasn't working on honing my technical skills, but I loved competing. The games were fun, and I was so good that I got asked to play often. All the players on my team were black; mine was one of a few white faces on the court. Here in Cape Cod, it didn't seem like an issue; everyone was civil. I didn't even realize an imbalance until one of the referees pointed it out.

I stood on the sidelines, laughing at one of my teammates' yo-mama jokes.

"Hey, you better get over there," he said, pointing toward half-court. "The other white boy's waiting for you."

The ref stood with the ball under one arm, his foot tapping impatiently. He shook his head at me as I jogged to half-court, disgust written all over his face.

"Sorry," I said. "I didn't realize—"

"How do you play ball with all these niggers?" he asked.

I was floored, stunned speechless. Just a moment ago I'd thought maybe I'd found the one place on earth where I could be both black and white without having to choose sides. Now this—a reminder that there was no such place. I let the awkward silence linger, then tossed him a sarcastic comeback. "It's tough, but someone has to do it."

Playing pickup did more than give me an outlet to play competitive hoops. The guy who ran one of the teams owned a bar, and he gave me a job as a bouncer a few nights a week.

Bouncing was easy money. I had no obligations during the day, so I could hang out, play ball, or just sit on the beach as long as I wanted. A couple of nights a week I went to the bar and stood around, looking menacing. Free dinner was one of the perks, and I got to socialize with everyone that came through the door. The whole summer was a blast.

Suzanne didn't tell her parents about the living situation; they didn't know I was at the house. Living with a girlfriend didn't feel any different than living at college, but she was worried about the perception even though we shared the house with four other people. The few times they visited the summer house, I cleared out until they left.

At the end of the summer, I went back home for ten days to change out some stuff, say hello, and get ready for junior year. As soon as I could, I got the hell out of there. Father Time had forgotten our house existed. Nothing had changed for the better; in fact, everything seemed to have gotten worse. Drugs and paraphernalia littered the place. I found pipes and residue everywhere. Mom seemed scattered and disoriented. Her appearance was disheveled, and she had gained a lot of weight. She walked much slower now; her gait had become an awkward, lumbering shuffle under the physical strain of her increased mass. With all the extra pounds, she didn't look like a stereotypical crackhead, so I stayed in denial. She still made it to work every day for both jobs while smoking like a chimney, but she drifted further away emotionally. Dad was his manic self. The two of them barely interacted. Everything was normal—or what passed for normal in living with them. They lived in the moment every moment, as though nothing could hurt them. Their lives were an elaborate game of Russian roulette.

I wanted to understand their behavior, but I never lectured, and I stayed away from the hard questions. Even after nineteen years, I was uncomfortable talking about drugs, so I asked about the cigarettes.

"Don't you know smoking is bad for you?" I asked Mom on one of the rare occasions I caught her between shifts.

She sighed. "I know, Devin." She held the butt of a still-lit cigarette between two fingers and tapped a fresh one out of the pack with her other hand.

I watched her light the new one with the embers of the old. "Then why do you keep doing it?"

"I'm trying to quit."

"Doesn't look like it."

Mom sighed again and rubbed her hand over her forehead. She looked exhausted. "You don't understand. I've been smoking for a long time. It's hard."

"You're killing yourself."

She ignored me.

"Isn't that important enough to do something different?"

No matter what I said, Mom had an excuse. It was obvious she didn't want to change, so I left it as it was and went back to campus as soon as I could. Every time I went back to school, it was tougher to come back to face the mess at home. No matter how much I wanted things to be different, my parents were too comfortable with the status quo. Their house became a motel where I crashed when I had nowhere else to go; it was no longer a home. I had no home.

CHAPTER 21

SPIRAL

FOR OUR JUNIOR YEAR, JOHN AND I RENTED HALF A HOUSE WITH TWO OTHER GUYS FROM THE BASKETBALL TEAM.

Jack Rupert and John were white, Jay Armstrong was black, and I was still somewhere in the middle, trying to figure it out. Once again, I didn't buy books for my fall schedule. When I walked through the doors for my first class that semester, my GPA hovered at 2.2, barely meeting the terms of my athletic eligibility. If my academic career was a swim meet, everyone else was racing and I was doggy-paddling in the deep end, wondering when it was all going to be over.

I went to classes intermittently, just enough to stay on my professors' radar screens. Upper-level classes at Colgate hit maximum capacity at twenty-five students. Professors knew everyone by name, and absences were obvious. None of my teachers ever asked me what was going on or tried to intervene with my lack of commitment. Without a strong guiding voice holding me accountable, I drifted. I approached class the same way I had approached Dad's trip through the religious buffet—get in, smile, nod, keep moving.

As the weeks dragged on, my grades spiraled out of control. I couldn't see or feel any consequences for my poor marks. At this point, I was in my third out of four years of my athletic eligibility, but I felt like I was waiting for something to begin. I felt like I hadn't really done anything. I had potential and I hadn't maxed out even once.

The only class that intrigued me that semester was sociology. The professor was a black man named Dr. Roy Bryce-Laporte. One of the topics we explored was the societal links between poverty and prison. Part of the coursework was a field trip to a prison.

Twenty-five of us piled into a few of the university's vans for the short trip to the correctional facility. Excited chatter filled the vehicle. No one else had been to a prison before. I joined in the banter as if the experience were new to me, too—but I so clearly remembered being pressed between inmates in the backseat of Dad's Buick, watching Dad's dancing dark eyes in the rearview mirror.

As soon as the vans passed the initial checkpoint, the students fell silent. I was the last one out of our van as the professor shepherded us into a tightly packed group. He gestured with a clipboard as he rattled through a list of rules for us to follow.

"Remember, the inmates are not allowed to talk to you. Do not engage them in conversation." He paused to give us a meaningful look. "Everybody's got it?"

We all looked at him. No one said anything. A feeling of nervous anticipation settled over us.

"All right then. Stay together."

The class moved like an amoeba; one edge of the group took a few steps, and everyone else followed along close behind. The first thing I noticed when we walked in the door was the noise. After the quiet outside, every sound seemed to echo inside those walls. Some of my peers jumped at every set of footsteps that approached. Quick, jittery smiles flitted through the group when a short scream reverberated from somewhere deep inside the facility.

The professor checked us all in with the wardens.

Up to this point, I had felt comfortable with the routine. However, as we congregated at the doorway into the medium-security wing, I felt myself get caught by the same spirit of tense expectation as my classmates. Two guards stood on either side of our professor; one of them was our official tour director, but I couldn't tell them apart. Two more guards brought up the rear of the group.

"The block you are about to enter is populated by prisoners convicted of gang-related activity," the tour guide's voice boomed. "The prison is currently overcrowded, as you'll see very clearly in a moment." He signaled to the uniforms keeping watch over the door.

I shifted my weight from foot to foot as we waited for the door to be unlocked. My classmates constricted into an even tighter group.

The tour leader turned his attention back to us. "The majority of the inmates are out in the yard. Those you see inside are restricted from yard privilege."

As soon as we entered the block, our professor jumped in with statistics. "Ninety percent of the prisoners in this wing …"

I tuned him out as the heavy door banged shut, sealing us inside. The room we stood in was a giant communal space. Cots were shoved up against the walls and packed in tight next to each other. There was hardly enough room to walk between them. Personal space was at a premium.

The class teetered on edge as we tiptoed around the edge of the room. A few prisoners peered at us. Like feral dogs, their eyes tracked our every movement. They projected an air of danger. One of them looked about my age. *How did you end up in here?* I wanted to talk to him, to hear his story.

As a whole, the class shied away from the inmates. I trailed behind the group to differentiate myself; I wanted the inmates to know I wasn't some rich kid here to see the show, or to look down on or judge them. The inmates could have reached out and grabbed one of us by the sleeve if they wanted to. It was like we were at a zoo, safe while the guards separated us from the prisoners, but what happened after lights-out?

The guide waited for everyone to rendezvous at the other end of the room. "Next we will take you past the yard. If any of the inmates attempt to engage you in conversation, just keep walking. You will stay with the rest of the group."

We didn't need the reminder.

The professor piped up again. He stood on his toes to try to project his voice to all of us. "The path you're walking now is one that the inhabitants of this cellblock walk once a day. Outside of work programs, this is the only time of day they spend outside the walls of the facility."

A rush of cool air enveloped me as we stepped outside to the yard. Contained by a chain-link and barbed-wire fence, a sea of faces looked out at us. They congregated around weight benches, watching each other pump iron as they waited for their turn at the equipment. Muscles popped and gleamed with sweat in the sunlight. A clear division ran down the center of the yard: the inmates isolated themselves by race. Black faces dominated one side, white ones the other. A bare patch of ground between them served as no-man's land. I watched the convicts as our professor and the guards kept up a tag-team lecture. No one stepped near the disputed ground.

My mind drifted as I searched the faces before us. If I were on the other side of this fence, where would I fit in? The white inmates looked nothing like the J. Crew crowd I ran with at Colgate. These guys were tough, with a weathered, broken-in look. There were a few skinheads interspersed in the mix. Despite my looks, I would definitely be on the side without the Aryan Nazi brotherhood.

The black side of the yard conjured memories of people from my past. Again, I identified with the group I looked nothing like. Even though I was intrigued by the contrast, how was I supposed to understand how the inmates got here by observing them from a distance? How did looking at where they slept and how they isolated themselves in the yard help us understand anything about them? Like the hookers on 14th Street, they had made their own choices, but I didn't know what had *driven* them in those directions. Did it even matter? I thought so. I was starting to believe that intent was everything, and that we were not a product of our environments, but our expectations.

Although that class caught my attention, the rest of my courses were a constant struggle. The worst was another sociology class. The professor was tough on me. Granted, I was as present as a mannequin in her classroom, but even when I tried, she shot me down.

I don't know whether it was racial, or because I was an athlete, or because I was oblivious during most of her lectures, but she seemed to have something against me personally.

As an experiment, Suzanne and I wrote similar papers for one of her assignments. I didn't copy any of her work, but we wrote about similar themes and I worked hard to make my prose readable. We both thought I'd done a good job.

The professor handed our papers back at the beginning of class a few weeks later. A big black C- dominated the top third of my paper. Suzanne's assignment received a B. I knew I was doing poorly, but I didn't need this woman ripping off the scab and pounding my already aching academic muscles. She stood at the front of the room, talking about the assignments. I raised my hand, a rare occasion.

The professor sighed. "Yes, Devin?" She looked at me as if I were holding up the class. There was no warm, fuzzy feeling of encouragement like I remembered from my tutors. This woman was geared up and ready for a confrontation.

I backed down. "Nothing."

What was I going to say? Despite my *belief* that she was biased, I had no ground to stand on when it came to arguing my academic merit. Undeserved or not, it was just another mediocre mark. What did it matter?

"Devin, it's not right," Suzanne said after class. "You deserve the same grade I do. You should go to talk to her during office hours. Or maybe even the dean. It's not—"

"It's fine." We walked with our heads tucked down on

the brisk fall day. "Who cares? It's not going to keep me from graduating. All I need's that diploma."

"Yeah, and then what?" Suzanne asked, only half teasing. She was an education minor and already knew she wanted to be a teacher. I had no clue what I was going to do post-Colgate.

"Come on." I nudged her playfully. "You know I'll figure it out. I'm still here, aren't I?"

Suzanne gave me a sidelong glance, trying not to smile. "I guess so."

"I have to get to practice," I said, giving her a quick kiss on the cheek. "The new coach is really riding me."

To replace Coach Baker, Colgate brought in Jack Bruen, who had coached Catholic University in DC. Hope, cloaked in skepticism, permeated the preseason pickup games.

"Bruen thinks we've got a chance in hell this year," one of the guys said, going for a layup. "He must not know what he's getting himself into."

By now, the team was immersed in a toxic losing culture. We were used to empty stands, to getting the pulp beat out of us. Our expectations had shifted, sunk so low that any implication we could come back—become winners—seemed not just ludicrous but naïve. For my part, even though I'd decided to stick with basketball, I'd become jaded. I was faking it. I had enough talent to ensure I wasn't the slowest antelope in the savannah, but I had no interest in becoming the fastest. Coach Bruen had different ideas for me—ideas he let me know loud and clear after every game.

We filed into the locker room after another loss. My

right knee hurt so bad I couldn't put my full weight on it, but I tried to hide my limp. *Show no weaknesses.* I'd started the game, but Coach Bruen took me out early in the fourth quarter.

"Do you care at all?" he yelled now. He gripped his clipboard so hard his knuckles turned white.

"Of course I care."

He narrowed his eyes. "You were one of the stars of St. John's. What happened to you?"

I shrugged.

The rest of the team edged away from us.

"What's the matter, Devin?" He got right in my face. His breath smelled like disappointment. "You scared?"

"No, Coach." I shifted my weight, trying to ease the pressure on my knee. I didn't know when I'd hurt it, but it was killing me. "I guess I just wasn't on top of my game tonight."

"You're scared, Devin." He stalked away, throwing his parting words over his shoulder like a casual alley-oop. "You could do more. You've got it in you, but you're choosing not to. You're a pansy."

I could tell his words came from a good place; he wanted me to succeed. The problem was that I would take his challenges to heart for a few days, but when I gave it a better effort, the pain in my knee flared. Something was wrong; I could feel it in the way the joint moved, in the sickening crackle of the connective tissues that accompanied every step. Still, I didn't tell anyone. The team kept losing.

By the start of second semester, my knee wasn't the only thing that was failing. An envelope containing a single sheet of official Colgate letterhead showed up in my mailbox one cold January afternoon.

Dear Mr. Hughes,

In an effort to help you achieve academic success, you are receiving this warning letter. Any student receiving less than a 2.0 GPA for two successive semesters will be placed on academic probation. Based on posted grades and past academic performance, you have been placed on academic probation effective as of the end of the fall semester.

The words bled together on the page. I had to read it three times before I understood: if I didn't get my grades up for spring semester, I'd forfeit my athletic eligibility and my spot on a Division I team. Without the scholarship, I couldn't afford school. I loved Colgate, but all the baggage from my childhood reappeared like Freddy Krueger. In the marathon that was college, I was at mile marker twenty-two; I was so close to the end I could almost see it, but I was dying on my feet. I called the one person I knew who could help.

"Mom?" I said when she answered the phone.

She knew right away something was wrong. "What's going on?"

It sucked being vulnerable, especially knowing that I had gotten myself into this mess by my own lack of initiative, but I knew Mom would fight, scratch, and claw to keep me in school.

"Devin? Are you still there?"

"Yeah." I took a deep breath and tapped the warning letter against the phone. "I need help."

"With what?"

"My grades."

Mom drove up to campus a few days later. That letter had scared me into going to every one of my classes, but I still didn't feel like I was learning anything. She asked me a ton of questions before she went to meet the deans. I told her about my sociology professor and the C- assignment.

"Do you still have that paper?"

I shuffled through a stack of crumpled papers on my desk.

Mom grabbed it out of my hands as soon as I found it. Her eyes flew left to right as she scanned the words. "Well, this is just ridiculous." She looked at me over the top of the paper. "I'm taking this to the dean."

She did exactly that. She was only on campus for two days, but she met with both deans; Dean Rice was black, and she won him over to our side right away. Even the white dean had to admit that my assignment was worthy of more than a C- as a final grade. After she talked to them alone, I had to face them as well.

Dean Rice was a personable guy. His smile put me at ease right away. I didn't know what she'd said to him in their previous meeting, but he was in my corner.

"So, Devin, your mom tells me you're capable of a lot more than what we've seen so far."

"Yes, sir," I answered. His office was huge compared to the coach's quarters. Giant windows framed either side of his desk. Mom and I sat across from him.

"You know …" He leaned forward, and the springs in the base of his chair creaked with his shift of weight. "If you can pull off 3.0s for your final three semesters, I can guarantee you'll get accepted at Syracuse Law."

I looked over at Mom, but her face was unreadable. Had she discussed law school with him? Where had this idea come from? A flicker of hope stirred in my chest. How hard could it be to pull a 3.0?

"We want you to succeed at Colgate. There are resources available if you need some help." He pushed a sheet of paper across the desk.

"Thanks." I took the paper, but his motivation didn't hit home. At that point, Nelson Mandela himself could have come up and talked to me and I would have given him the same head nod. I just had to get my diploma. That was all that mattered.

After those meetings with the dean, I improved enough to get off probation, but I still wasn't an academic rock star. The flare of hope about Syracuse Law faded faster than a cough drop; the 3.0 eluded me. I bought all the books for spring semester, but I didn't open them often. Resorting to my elementary school tricks, I read enough to memorize and regurgitate the information on exams, and forgot almost everything shortly afterward.

As basketball season drew to a close, I iced my knee nonstop. I kept trying to push through the pain, but it throbbed like a headache right under the kneecap. I told my roommates, but as college athletes, we were all used to hurting physically. With only five games remaining in the season, I couldn't take it anymore. After a close game, which we lost, I limped back to the locker room with my teammates. My right leg dragged behind. It hurt so bad I didn't care whether I looked weak.

A couple of the other starting string players walked right in front of me. Their voices were a rush of angry mutters. I caught my name in their hushed conversation.

"Man, did you see Devin just quit out there?"

"How are we ever supposed to win if our starters give up?"

I was floored. The locker room door almost hit me in the shoulder. Obviously the team had noticed my problems, but they thought I just didn't care. Before I even knew what I was doing, I stopped the conversation around me. A couple of my teammates surrounded me, kicking off shoes and peeling off sweat-soaked jerseys.

"Look, guys," I said. "I feel like I let the team down."

The mutters and shoe-kicking stopped. All eyes turned to me. Time to throw myself on the land mine.

"I know this season we haven't really gotten what we wanted, but I'm not giving up." I took a deep breath. "I've been playing hurt all year. I should've told someone I needed a break, but we're so close to the end of the season now, I'm going to push through."

Silence. The din of the rest of the team packing it in roared in the background. I warmed to the speech. It felt good, cathartic, to open myself up to the guys. "I promise you this: for the next game and in the tournament, I will bring my A-game against Hartford. I will give it everything, leave everything on the floor, and all I ask is that you do the same."

The guys glanced at one another. Heads nodded.

A few of them cracked smiles. I could feel their energy levels rising and almost couldn't believe it: they were responding to my words.

"Wherever we end up, we end up, but I need us to stay together and take down Hartford. We can do it. *We* just need to believe it. Okay?"

"All right, Dev," one of the guys said with a nod. He looked around. "We're with you."

The tension that had been in the air lifted almost immediately after my impromptu speech. Soon the locker room was full of the usual noises—showers running, the metallic clank of locker doors slamming. Laughter rose, and I caught snippets of conversation about us beating Hartford. As I showered up and changed, I relished in the feeling of what I had just done. I had stood in front of a crowd—albeit a small one—without knowing what I was going to say, laid my weaknesses bare, and *inspired* them. I felt as though I'd stumbled upon some secret power. I wanted more.

First, though, I needed to take care of my knee. We had two weeks before heading to the North Atlantic Conference tournament. That following Monday, I went to see Marty Erb, the Colgate trainer.

I limped into his office and immediately sat down. "Marty, I can't do this anymore."

"What do you mean?" Marty slid my way in his wheeled chair.

I propped my leg on the chair across me, rolling up my pants leg. Marty prodded and poked, had me bend and straighten the joint.

"You have got to get off of this leg," he said after a

few minutes. "You're going to have to sit out until we can figure out what's going on."

Relief washed over me, tinged with guilt. "But I've got to practice," I argued weakly.

"Do you want to practice, or do you want to play? Keep practicing like this and your playing days are over."

For the next ten days, I watched my team practice without me. Was I a pansy for not playing through the pain like I had all year? Thankfully, my knee started to feel better just in time for the conference tournament. We were playing Hartford on their home turf, in the Hartford Civic Center. They'd drilled us the last time we faced them. From the excitement in the home bleachers, it was obvious the fans expected an easy victory.

No one expected us to win.

My promise to my teammates hung over my head. I was well rested and fresh, ready to make good on delivering my A-game. The noise of the civic center roared as both teams lined up for tipoff. The ref threw the ball in the air. Time slowed to a crawl as I waited to see who would grab it. Hartford's forward jumped just a little higher and slapped the ball toward one of his teammates.

Suddenly I was in a dead sprint, back in real time. I followed the ball all the way down the court and jumped in for my first rebound. The pain I expected when I landed never came.

We flew down the court, the ball snapping from player to player as we worked our way around Hartford's starting lineup. I saw my opening, grabbed a pass, and put up my first shot. It *whooshed* through the net. I was on fire. I hadn't played this well since St. John's.

Who knew whether my speech had anything to do with it, but we were all on top of our game that night. My knee felt better than it had in months. I led the pack with eighteen points and nine rebounds; I was invincible.

The score waffled back and forth; neither team gained much of a lead. With one minute left, Hartford sank a basket to put themselves up by two. The stands went crazy. Everyone thought this was the end. My legs were exhausted, and my lungs screamed for oxygen. One more minute. We sprinted down the court toward our basket. I had the ball. The red numbers on the scoreboard counted down in the corner of my vision. It was now or never.

I ran up to the top of the key and took a three-point shot.

All the noise in the civic center fell away. For me, the only sound was the beat of my heart that thundered through my ears as the ball spun toward the basket. It bounced off the rim once; the entire arena gasped a collective breath. The ball sank through the rim. Three points. I won the game.

Hartford never saw it coming. Neither did we. That one win changed everything. Sealing the win felt like redemption for all the times I hadn't given it my all. Pride in coming through when the team needed it most was a feeling I sorely missed.

"If we win two more games, we're going to the NCAAs!" Coach said in the locker room. "I'm proud of you, Devin."

I basked in the recognition. We partied in our hotel rooms that night. Everyone was ecstatic. We dreamed with our eyes open. Winning that one game caused a complete one-eighty in the team's collective attitude toward our chances.

The next day, reality came back to meet us: after our upset against Hartford, the coach of the Boston University Terriers had prepared his players to face us. The game was never even close; we got blitzed. The dream that seemed so real only the day before was over. In what felt like minutes, our year was finished, but we went out on a much higher note than the previous year.

Shortly after the tournament, I took a trip home to see my doctor for the pain in my knee. His diagnosis was torn cartilage. I was relieved by the news; just like when I had been diagnosed with dyslexia, I didn't fully understand the problem, but if it had a name, I felt I could beat it.

"So what do we need to do?" I asked.

The doctor put his hands on either side of my knee-cap. "Well, we're going to have to go in and surgically remove the damaged piece." He pointed at a spot near the top of my knee.

Worry set in immediately at the word *surgery*. "What's recovery like? Will I be able to regain full strength and mobility?"

The doctor smiled. "We'll set up a physical therapy program for you after surgery. How much work you put into it in the coming months will be up to you."

Months? I did not want to miss my senior season. "If we do it now, will I be ready to go by October?"

"I'd say with a little dedication you could be back on your feet playing ball in six months."

In April, I went into surgery thinking I'd wake up with an ace bandage to stabilize my knee. Instead, a huge immobilizer kept my entire leg still. Fire roared through my veins. My knee hurt worse than ever. For a second, I was struck with shock and fear—what if this was it? What if I never played or, hell, never *walked* without pain again?

Just then, the doctor walked past my room and saw that I was awake. "Hey, by the way, I thought it was just cartilage, but it was more serious than we thought. You had a partial tear of your patellar tendon."

My whole knee pulsed; it was as though I could feel every torn fiber of that tendon. "How long will the pain last?"

"That will subside gradually over the next few weeks. I'll give you a prescription for some medication that will help you manage the pain."

The pills weren't strong enough; I popped them like candy, but they barely took the edge off. I stayed at my parents' house for a couple of days, but I had a lot of work waiting for me at Colgate. The academic ultimatum still loomed over my head. With my leg immobilized, I couldn't drive, and both of my parents had to work, so I was forced to take the train by myself.

I boarded the Amtrak at Union Station in DC. It was tough. I was in a lot of pain and couldn't get around well on the crutches. The long ride through New York gave me plenty of time to think about the three years I'd wasted, both on and off the court. My college career was a rotten sandwich stuffed with mediocrity, and I couldn't get the taste out of my mouth. I had no idea what I wanted to do in the future; until I hurt my knee, I hadn't looked all that far ahead. With nothing to do now but think, I realized that my life had no direction. I wanted to be a success, but I didn't know how to get there. Now that the season was over, I had time to spend on physical therapy … and focusing on passing all my classes.

CHAPTER 22

PROGRESS

THE SUMMER AFTER JUNIOR YEAR WAS UNEVENTFUL.

I couldn't find a job or go out because I couldn't get around on my own. My only focus was rehabbing my knee. Fortunately, Mom had worked her way up to management at a physical therapy facility owned by an orthopedic surgeon. The doctor was also the physician for the Washington Bullets, so his therapists were familiar with sports-related injuries.

Treatment for my leg involved a lot of stretching and strength training. The repair work on the tendon left behind a lot of scar tissue that needed to be broken up and reintroduced to hard use. I had to ride in with Mom, so I was stuck there all day. She created part-time work for me so I could earn a little spending money. Every day, Monday through Friday, I spent a few hours filing and answering phones while Mom ran the office. She managed the entire facility, including the patients and employees.

Seeing her in action was fantastic. In this environment, she was upbeat, positive, and energetic. She smiled and laughed frequently. In every interaction with other people she was engaging and personable; she seemed utterly delighted to be there in that moment. This was the side of her I had only seen glimpses of before. We ate lunch together every day; sometimes we went out for lunch at a local diner just around the corner, and sometimes we had food delivered. We hadn't spent this much time together in my entire life. She was in a good place. She liked having me around, and I enjoyed every minute I spent in the rehab clinic.

I spent mornings doing a little office work and focusing on my knee exercises. Rehab was a slow process.

I couldn't run after surgery; I couldn't even walk at a fast pace. To reclaim the strength and flexibility needed for basketball I had to work on lateral movements and stair stepping the entire three months. After a few weeks of the routine, I was bored. It felt like I wasn't doing anything to make myself stronger. I started pumping weights like crazy just to have something to do. The effects showed. My arms and chest bulked up with new muscle that I couldn't help but admire—thirty-five pounds of it. In my narrow field of vision I lost site of the fact that basketball players needed to be lean in order to run and jump effectively.

My knee wasn't completely healed by the start of fall semester, but I was at least able to drive myself to campus in September. This year, John and I were sharing an apartment two miles from Colgate; we were ready for new surroundings. This was the first year I didn't think about my identity or where I fit in ethnically. I wasn't hanging around that many black guys, except on the team, and my girlfriend and all my best friends were white. It wasn't a conscious decision, but I lived out that year as part of the white college culture.

A couple guys from the team dropped by while we were moving in; everyone was curious about my knee.

"Dude. Your arms are enormous."

"What did you *do* all summer?"

I preened and flexed. "Lifted weights a little. No big deal. I had to do something while I was waiting for my knee to heal."

"Yeah, but you're *huge.* Aren't you afraid that'll slow you down?"

I shrugged. Now that someone had pointed it out, I couldn't see why I hadn't realized the potential downside.

"Are you ready to practice with us now?"

"No," I said. I tried not to notice the worried looks on my teammates' faces. "But I'm going to be on court for the first official practice."

The NCAA mandated that the first day of regular practice be October 15. I still had a month and a half to rehab, and I was determined to make it. This was my senior year. I wanted to be a part of the team from the beginning. I focused on my goal, and worked hard toward it.

At first, I played a limited role. A combination of strength and stretching exercises with the training staff was all I was cleared to do; I wasn't allowed any contact. Slowly, I worked my way up to jogging on my own. The improvements over the previous season became obvious. For the first time in over a year, I felt no pain in my knee. I put enough work in that my knee was strong enough to get out on the court that first day.

The first day of practice felt like a fresh start. We were all optimistic and eager to conquer the world. Coach Bruen ran us through drills during the first workout. The shrill of his whistle sent us pounding down the court in sprints. After two heats I fell way behind. I had gained so much weight, and even though it was all muscle, it was a lot to carry around. The lack of cardio training showed.

Coach Bruen frowned as I jogged by. "Been a tough summer, Devin?"

I didn't answer. My lungs were burning. I put my hands on my thighs and gasped for air.

After practice, the coach announced that year's captains. Captains were always senior players, and only two of us were starters. I thought I stood a good chance, but Bruen announced two other names. One of his selected captains didn't even play; he had more time on the bench last year than any other guy on the team.

I was pissed. If I was honest with myself, I hadn't really put in the effort to earn the position, but I could have. I waited around after practice ended, thinking Coach Bruen might explain why he hadn't picked me. He was the last one out of the locker room.

"See you tomorrow, Devin," he said.

That stung. This was my last year at Colgate, the culmination of my college career, and I didn't have the leadership role I wanted.

Our first game was in November against Oklahoma State. We flew down to Stillwater, ready to turn over a new leaf. This was Bruen's second year coaching, and we held on to the hope that we could somehow turn our team around. I was in the starting lineup. I wasn't in the greatest shape, but I was ready to go.

I shook hands with Byron Houston, an all-American on the Cowboys' team. He was my height, maybe a little taller. We battled through the whole game; I even threw him to the floor once. After the first quarter I knew putting on the extra thirty-five pounds of muscle was a big mistake. I couldn't keep up; the weight killed my quickness.

Despite our best efforts, the Cowboys beat us by forty points. We weren't emotionally ready for the loss. A couple guys joked about our perpetual losing streak after the game.

Coach Bruen flipped out. "This is college basketball, not some casual game of Saturday morning three-on-three. Act like it." He stomped away in disgust. "You're bunch of pansies—weak little pansies."

Compared to previous years, I put in more effort during practices than I had throughout the rest of my college career. Between practices, however, I didn't put in any extra work. I didn't spend my time working on my game. I played, but put no effort into improving my game. From childhood through college, working on my game wasn't a habit I'd developed. If I wanted to be great, I had to put in the extra time, but I didn't. I didn't love basketball enough. I loved the spotlight, but when no one was around I couldn't motivate myself to go to the gym and shoot. Unless I had a destination in mind, unless I could connect the dots between the work and getting to another place, I wouldn't do it.

After losing our first few games, we all fell back into the expectation that we were losers. I never went into a game thinking we would win. The guys on the team all got along but it wasn't a close-knit group. We didn't have the collective spirit and morale necessary to pull us through the tough times together, so we fell apart.

"Man, I'm out of here," one of the black players said with disgust after we'd been trounced for the seventh straight game.

"Maybe if he ever let us play it wouldn't be so bad,"

one of his friends said.

"Whatever. I'm done with this."

A few of the black players quit in January. They accused Coach Bruen of racism, but I was sure it was just an excuse to get out of the losing culture. I couldn't blame them.

I stuck it out. The end was in sight for both basketball and school. Over the course of the past month the realization had started to sink in that I would probably leave Colgate never having given anything my best effort. I was wasting my potential. Instead of working harder and using that as motivation, I spiraled further into self-pity and doubt. As we continued to lose I started getting more anxious and more stressed out about my own mediocre performance.

At one of our last games I stood at half-court with one of my teammates just before the start of the third quarter. Our cheering section was more than half empty. I was frustrated; I knew I wasn't playing as well as I could. I didn't want my college basketball career to end on such a morose note, but it was too late to change it. The forward from the opposing team ran up and laughed at us.

"You clowns. We're drilling you." He pointed his finger at my teammate's face. "You're soft." He kept talking trash at my teammate.

I watched, all the emotions and frustrations I'd compartmentalized all year bubbling inside my veins. The weight of four years of disappointment fell on me like a ton of wet sand. I hadn't taken advantage of a single opportunity I'd been offered in my entire college career.

The long fuse that had been burning all semester finally reached its end. All my frustrations exploded outward in fury.

I snapped, grabbing the guy by his jersey and hauling him to the bleachers.

"What the hell—"

Chaos erupted on the court. I ignored everything and everyone around me and pushed the forward down to the ground. I slammed him into the stands, about to hit him. Someone tried to grab me from behind so I turned and grasped that person by the shirt, slamming him into the stands. The black and white stripes of the referee's jersey disappeared from sight as he crumpled to the ground and a swarm of people tried to pull everyone apart.

I stood there like an outsider watching my own body. In my mind, I saw my dad hauling that white guy out of the stands at the high school football game so many years ago. It was odd, but familiar.

We lost the game, as usual. I expected a lecture about my behavior, but Coach Bruen wasn't mad.

"I'm proud of you for standing up for your teammate," he said.

I shrugged. I wished I could say that it was the act of chivalry that my coach believed it to be, but at that moment I just needed to scream.

After coming to the realization that I'd wasted my time at school, I didn't try to kick it into high gear for the next few months to finish off strong. I didn't know how. I'd bitten down hard on this sandwich of mediocrity and I didn't have a toothpick sharp enough to dig it out of my teeth. Once again, all I knew was that I had to graduate.

We lost our final game against Holy Cross. My basketball career was over. I would never play competitive basketball again. I stood there under our basket, amidst a sea of people and somehow alone. Players from Holy Cross jumped and hollered all around me. The Colgate side of the stands was quiet, but a constant, dull roar assailed us from the victors' side. My teammates filed past me, heads down, in the same losing posture we'd assumed for four years. My heart pounded. I couldn't move. Was this my legacy?

I finally found my feet and shuffled to the locker room. At best, our team had won a quarter of our games in four years. I'd been handed a golden ticket because of my natural ability and I wasted it. The locker room echoed with the hollow banging of metal doors. One of the younger players rushed past me and banged into my shoulder in his rush to leave, but I barely noticed. The team was already drifting apart.

The smell of sweat and disappointment was like a wet towel wrapped around my head, muffling the world and choking my breath. I walked past the banks of lockers and my dejected teammates. If anyone said anything to me, I didn't hear it. I found the farthest corner of the room, put my back to the wall, and slid down to the floor.

Four years of failure pressed down on my shoulders. Sobs wracked my body before I even realized I was crying. I needed a course correction; I couldn't live my life like this, always doing the bare minimum to stay afloat. College was supposed to be where the magic happened, where my life changed, but all I felt was a lack of direction and no clarity of purpose. I had spent the last four years running from my parents' example, never realizing I had followed right in their footsteps.

It was too late to save my track record in school, but I could look forward. Suzanne was still on track toward becoming a teacher. She was supportive and encouraging through that final semester; she knew I was frustrated. I wanted to stay with her, but we hadn't ever talked about what would happen in June. I was heading back to DC after graduation, because that was the only place I knew as home. Questions about how to get a job after school bounced around in my head, but I didn't know how to start those conversations. My focus was on limping my way through to graduation and collecting the diploma.

I was going to graduate fifth from the bottom out of more than seven hundred. The main disappointment was that it wasn't due to my lack of capability. I just never gave it my best effort. Not trying gave me a built-in excuse for failure.

What do I want to be when I grow up? I went to the library to research what different industries paid. Until this point, I had never thought about what job I wanted. I hadn't interned, didn't have a resume, and I was too intimidated to go to the career center because of my grades. Instead of making myself vulnerable and asking for help, I ran the other direction and tried to figure it out myself.

I looked up service manager jobs, call centers, and

hotel management, anything that I could somewhat relate to or see in my realm of experience. Physical therapy was a brief daydream until I found out I'd have to apply to graduate school. The consequences of my subpar effort hit me. *How did I not see this?* I had never connected the dots between grades and my life as a college graduate. All my dreams of success crumbled around me. I had closed doors for myself without meaning to. I'd had so many great classes and exceptional professors, and I hadn't engaged myself in the experience. Regret flooded my thoughts during every waking moment. I didn't mention it to Suzanne or to any of my friends. Bulletproof—that was the façade I felt compelled to maintain.

Even though I didn't take full advantage of the resources at Colgate, I had learned about other people's perspectives of the world, and about getting along with people of different cultures and ethnicities. In some ways, I felt as though I had left my black identity back in DC. I knew it was there; when I was back in that environment, I put those shoes on, and at Colgate I took them off again. What would happen if I returned to DC more permanently? What identity would I slip into?

"What are you going to do after graduation?" John asked me out of the blue one afternoon.

"Be a success," I quipped. It was April. Most of the senior class was busy lining up jobs or wrapping up internships. I relied on my wit and sarcasm to get me around the tough conversations. "Successful" was my go-to answer any time somebody asked me what I wanted to be.

The night before graduation, all of my buddies' parents came to town. My parents were up as well, staying at the Colgate Inn. John threw on a nice shirt and checked himself out in the mirror. He was meeting his parents for a dinner my friends had been planning for weeks.

"Are you sure your parents don't want to come along tonight? David, Matt, and Jeff's parents are all going, too."

"Nah," I lied. "They're not getting here until late."

John shrugged. "Suit yourself. See you later."

"Bye."

The truth was that I'd never even told my parents about the dinner. I hadn't seen them in months; I didn't know if Dad was on his meds or if Mom was clean. Throwing Dad into the mix with my white friends and their white parents didn't sound like a good idea. My friends all knew Dad was black, but they had never met him. Plus, I still didn't have any idea what I would do after college ended, and I didn't want to listen to everybody's parents gush about their kids' blossoming career paths.

When my parents got into town, I headed over to the hotel to meet them. Mom had gained even more weight, and Dad was sillier than ever, but all things considered, they seemed reasonably fine.

"You're a college graduate now." Dad beamed. "There aren't any doors closed to you now."

Except grad school, law school, or competitive athletics. I mustered a faint smile and didn't tell him he was wrong.

We ate at the hotel that night. I sat across from them, confronted head-on by the stark contrast between their skin colors. Whether at school or at home, I didn't have to face the convergence of these two worlds; I always chose one or the other. Having to admit that I couldn't ever separate them completely made me feel uncomfortable and alone. Dinner passed by in a fog. Wrapped up in my own internal crisis, I couldn't concentrate on anything going on around me. I went to bed dreading the morning.

Colgate University's one hundred and seventieth graduation ceremony was held on one of the large lawns at the heart of campus. My parents were somewhere in the crowd, but I didn't seek them out beforehand. The crowd of students buzzed with excitement around me, the barely organized chaos just waiting to burst forth into the real world.

"Can you believe it?" a girl behind me said to her friend.

"I can't believe it's over," her friend replied.

"Over? You start work in what, three weeks?"

Both girls laughed. All around me, students talked about their plans for the summer, for getting jobs, and for going to grad school. Every excited voice felt like a slap in the face. I cursed my limited foresight. At least I would have that magical diploma. With that in hand, at least I would have something to show for my time at Colgate. I scanned the crowd for Suzanne's face but couldn't find her.

I sat in an uncomfortable folding chair in the cap and gown, with the tassel brushing against my cheek in the spring breeze. The chair became lopsided as one leg sunk further into the grass than the others. Professors and university officials sat in a row on the stage before us. One by one, speakers walked up to the microphone and gave short speeches that seemed too long. Twenty minutes into it, the student body lost all interest. I couldn't sit still. The speaker introduced Senator Richard Lugar of Indiana for the graduation address.

Senator Lugar walked up to the microphone, a big politician's smile pasted on his face. He held an honorary Doctor of Law degree from the university in Hamilton. That put him in the ranks of the Rev. Dr. Samuel Proctor, the pastor emeritus of the Abyssinian Baptist Church in Harlem; Judith Jamison, artistic director of Alvin Ailey American Dance Theater; political commentator Kevin Phillips; E. Garrett Bewkes, the retiring chairman of the Colgate board; and Judy Woodruff, a correspondent for *The MacNeil/Lehrer NewsHour*.

No one cared about credentials. It was like Christmas morning, and Lugar stood between us and a big stack of presents. I didn't hear a thing he said.

When it came time to get our diplomas, I followed the people beside me like a windup doll. I trudged up to the stage, my eyes on the cap and gown in front of me.

"Congratulations," the dean said as I shook hands with him.

I mumbled my thanks and didn't look him in the eye. He was the one who had tried to tempt me with Syracuse Law. Did he know how bad my grades were?

I shook hands with everybody on stage, grabbed my

diploma, and headed back to my seat to wait for the rest of the graduating class to cycle through. I turned the diploma over in my hands, inspecting this one sheet of paper that was supposed to change my life. For so long I had counted on this diploma as the answer to all my problems. I didn't feel any different, just disappointed. My parents didn't seem to notice.

"My boy's a college grad," Dad said enthusiastically.

"Stand together," Mom directed, holding up a camera. "Smile, Devin."

I plastered a fake smile on my face, but I felt hollow, indifferent. My parents hugged me and smiled at everyone who passed by. Mom snapped pictures every few minutes. The last time they'd taken this many pictures of me was the first time I'd put on my St. John's ROTC uniform.

I made it through the rest of the day, but couldn't let go of the opportunity that I had wasted. The finality of knowing that I hadn't given it all I had wouldn't go away. Tomorrow I would pack my things and head back to DC. *To do what, exactly?* I lay on my bed and stared at the ceiling. I hadn't interned, didn't know how to interview, and didn't even know how to go about finding a job as a college graduate. All the negative self-talk left a bitter taste in my mouth.

On the road the next day, I had plenty of time to think. My life as a student and an athlete was over, but my future still lay ahead of me. Realization dawned like a set of bright headlights from an oncoming truck. I could mope about the past, or I could look forward and learn from the experience.

Dad's voice echoed back to me across the years. "You can either find a way or an excuse. We find a way. We survive."

If I kept telling myself *I can't*, of course I would continue to fail. If things were to get better, I needed to get better. If my life was to improve, I must improve. I glimpsed my eyes in the rearview mirror and it was like looking at my four-year-old self.

"I *am* somebody, I *can* do it, I *will* do it."

The words sounded loud in the quiet car. Memories of riding down the streets of DC on Dad's bike flew by in a whirlwind of images. Through all the setbacks of my childhood, he had tried to teach me to push through, to keep my head up and stay positive. If I could change my attitude, I could change my life; all I had to do was believe it.

AFTERWORD

For years, I tried to escape the feeling of being judged. Like most things you try to run from, however, it lingered in the background, always visible in my rearview mirror no matter how hard I tried not to look. Ten years after I graduated from Colgate, my mother passed away. I started to reflect on her life, and our lives, and I realized that in order for me to grow and evolve, I had to wrap my arms around the issues I'd tried so hard to leave behind.

By taking a step back and examining the past, I came to two realizations. One: my parents were flawed people. They made mistakes, but they never intentionally put me in harm's way. Dad did the best he could as a ninth-grade dropout without a role model for decent parenting; Mom stood up for me when it mattered, trying to help me avoid the path she couldn't seem to abandon. Being angry at them for their decisions wouldn't change my situation. I found that I could separate their actions from their intentions, and appreciate them for meaning well.

All my life, my parents told me I was destined for more. That's tough to believe when you're a kid. After struggling through school, I brushed all those thoughts away, but in reexamining Mom's life, I started to internalize the message. All those old conversations came back, and I realized she was right: I had something more to offer the world than what I'd been giving. When you feel you've been destined to put your fingerprints on the universe, you realize that you're not a by-product of your environment, but a by-product of your expectations. I could either dwell on my childhood experiences and let them consume me, or I could use them as a tool to show others that obstacles and adversity can be overcome.

The second realization I came to was the significance of self-talk. Dad used to tell me, "As good as you think you are, there is always somebody, somewhere, working a little bit harder. You can't control the referees; you can't control your teammates. What you can control is your attitude and your level of engagement." When you are alone, isolated, and don't feel like you can trust anyone, transform your mental soundtrack from "I'm not good enough, not smart enough" to "I am going to get through this. I am a good person. I will be okay tomorrow." I pulled myself through some tough situations with this kind of self-talk.

After Colgate, I knew that before I asked anyone to change, I had to do it for myself. I've changed and grown through the process of reconnecting with my past, to the point where I am finally comfortable with who I am. That person can't be defined by checking a box on a form.

I am not black. I am not white. I am me.

I earned the right to be at Colgate, and then didn't give it my best shot. The regret lingers. Don't give yourself the same easy out. Don't sit on the highway doing thirty miles an hour while everyone else zips by going seventy because you're afraid that your car isn't fast enough. Engage; get something out of every moment. I wasted a golden opportunity, athletically and academically, but that wasn't a death sentence. I learned from it and moved forward. Today, I work with schools and organizations of all kinds to turn around a lack of motivation and help people capitalize on their potential. No one knows more than me the frustration of self-sabotage.

I am not by any means done growing. My family relationships are still disjointed: I have not connected with my half brother and sister, and Dad's dad is ninety-six and there is still no connection there. Does this bother me? Yes, but I have learned not to carry all the baggage around with me. Even though I hit rock bottom in college, that provided the wake-up call I needed to start a change in my own life.

If you find yourself in a situation where you can either find a way or make an excuse, I hope my story inspires you to take the road less traveled. The world is an unbelievably exciting place if you let yourself live in it.

Be vulnerable, engage in each moment, and tell yourself you *can* do it. And remember: life is about progress, not perfection.

I'd love to hear about your experience reading *Contrast*. To contact me, please visit *www.devinchughes.com*, or call 888-964-1113.

CPSIA information can be obtained at www.ICGtesting.com
Printed in the USA
LVOW080917270612

287871LV00001B/1/P